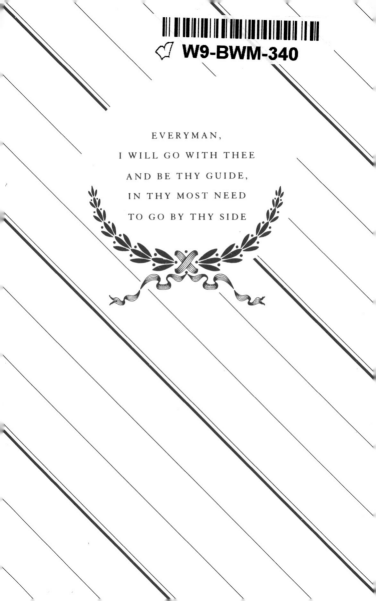

EVERYMAN,
I WILL GO WITH THEE
AND BE THY GUIDE,
IN THY MOST NEED
TO GO BY THY SIDE

EVERYMAN'S LIBRARY
POCKET POETS

From one psycho to
another — some
words to relate
to.
                n.

Beat Poets

Selected and edited by
Carmela Ciuraru

E V E R Y M A N ' S   L I B R A R Y

P O C K E T   P O E T S

Alfred A. Knopf · New York · Toronto

THIS IS A BORZOI BOOK
PUBLISHED BY ALFRED A. KNOPF

This selection by Carmela Ciuraru first published in
Everyman's Library, 2002
Copyright © 2002 by Everyman Publishers plc
A list of acknowledgments to copyright owners appears at the back
of this volume.

www.randomhouse.com/everymans

ISBN 0-375-41332-4

Typography by Peter B. Willberg
Typeset in the UK by AccComputing, North Barrow, Somerset
Printed and bound in Germany by GGP Media, Pössneck

CONTENTS

FOREWORD

Their language was dizzying, drunken, irreverent, tender, scatological, elegiac, and often hilarious. They were the Beats. Strictly speaking, the group comprised Allen Ginsberg, Jack Kerouac, William Burroughs, Neal Cassady, and Herbert Huncke, but the term also extended to intersecting groups of post–World War II American writers—among them poets of the San Francisco Renaissance, the Black Mountain School, and the New York School. Additionally, there were various hangers-on, wannabe bohemians, and so-called second-generation Beats—all disillusioned (but not cynical) young people struggling to redefine themselves, to discover sexual and political liberation and perhaps a new kind of faith. "Beat" was not just about a common aesthetic. It was also a lifestyle, a state of mind.

In his 1952 *New York Times Magazine* article "This Is the Beat Generation," John Clellon Holmes addressed the problems of labeling an entire generation, calling it "unrewarding," yet he acknowledged that his generation somehow "demands an adjective." And so he described the Beat Generation as one that implies

> the feeling of having been used, of being raw. It involves a sort of nakedness of mind, and ultimately, of soul: a feeling of being reduced to the bedrock of consciousness. In short, it means being undramatically pushed up against the wall

13

of oneself. A man is beat whenever he goes for broke and wagers the sum of his resources on a single number; and the young generation has done that continually from early youth.

Like punk, grunge, and most other countercultural trends, the avant-garde Beat movement—once serving as a rebellious, taunting cry against bourgeois intellectualism and repression—was soon snapped up by mainstream America. ("Kerouac opened a million coffee bars and sold a million pairs of Levis to both sexes," Burroughs once said of his friend.)

The Beats, and those affiliated with that core group, were mostly men, and the work they produced was almost entirely male-focused. It must be said that despite their progressive-mindedness—think of all those graphic poems about homosexual intercourse being written in the 1950s—Beat writings were often ridiculously misogynistic. Women were usually idealized (or demonized) as maternal figures, or else honored for their skills in bed. Although some of the more offensive poems read, fifty years later, almost like parodies—and some were surely intended as such—it would be misleading to edit them out of the story. To do so would be to produce a falsely tidy representation of the writings produced at that time.

A number of these poems are self-indulgent, sloppy, even at times incoherent. But the lesser poems—alongside such classics as Ginsberg's masterpiece, "Howl," or Corso's "Poets Hitchhiking on the Highway"—also define the Beat Generation. Some of these poems may fall short of traditional standards of literary quality, but overturning convention is partly what the spirit of that movement was about. Taken together, these works celebrate the marvelous individuality of the Beat poets —their utter refusal to be tamed by anyone. There is something admirable about that.

As for the disproportionate space given to certain poets over others, that's simply the result of editorial preferences. This anthology is not meant to serve as a comprehensive guide; it is intended to be, like so many anthologies, a primer, a starting place.

One final note: Beat poems *insist* upon being read aloud—preferably in the grand, self-dramatizing style that the Beats themselves often favored as they declaimed their poems in smoke-filled cafés and bars.

Whether you recite in front of an audience or read in solitude, you will absorb the jazzy rhythms of these poems and savor their exuberant, fractured music and despair.

CARMELA CIURARU

From POEMS OF MADNESS
"City Madness"

I used to sit often composing the manuscript
never denouncing and therefore not to be written
without preparation for trial.

I'd sit contemplating unobvious thoughts without poetry,
being the poet of adequate life
on broken brick steps full of contractions
of piles and pimply sores from the stone
and syphilis-eyed hypochondria sleep-thinking germs
bringing flu
and I caught my first cold fifteen histories ago
in the maggoty festering garbage-can alley
back of my mother's rear room.

I used to sit dreaming the dreams of accomplishment
marching in questionable cadences down to the foot
of the Harborside Terminal
into the emptying carrying cars of Spry and Colgate
Mullers outgoing spaghetti and infinite
meatballs!

counting the black-balled parolees and broken-backed
spics, Italian laborers, Polacks and sweaty
old terminal boss,
whose unknotted tie and left-wide-agape collar
was motive enough to imagine the noose.

When I was ten I discovered the poet and quick
circulated great novels of spy and adventure
and killer police, whose murderous face
I didn't at first grasp
until I discovered a cop humping some young
indiscernible girl in the park.

She addressed him with delicate fits from her lips
which turned ghosty and blue and the dress tore away
and he popped with a joy every cop in New Jersey recalls.

Since then I have hated what passes as law
and the ten-year-old grew but the poet did not
and the novels fell off into idiot poems
and madness and sight of my city,
the city of squares and the city of Pharisees
all mobbed into a mass of the lewdest advertisement,
tight denim levis—buck shoes for the silent
and cardigan jitterbug jackets with saddle stitched
     pockets
of rubber . . .

HELLO

It is disastrous to be a wounded deer.
I'm the most wounded, wolves stalk,
and I have my failures, too.
My flesh is caught on the Inevitable Hook!
As a child I saw many things I did not want to be.
Am I the person I did not want to be?
That talks-to-himself person?
That neighbors-make-fun-of person?
Am I he who, on museum steps, sleeps on his side?
Do I wear the cloth of a man who has failed?
Am I the looney man?
In the great serenade of things,
      am I the most canceled passage?

From ODE TO COIT TOWER

O anti-verdurous phallic were't not for your pouring
    height looming in tears like a sick tree or your
    ever-gaudy-comfort jabbing your city's much
    wrinkled sky you'd seem an absurd Babel squatting
    before mortal millions

Because I filled your dull sockets with my New York
    City eyes vibrations that hadn't doomed dumb
    Empire State did not doom thee

Enough my eyes made you see phantasmal at night mad
    children of soda caps laying down their abundant
    blond verse on the gridiron of each other's euchar-
    istic feet like distant kings laying down treasures
    from camels

Illuminations hinged to masculine limbs fresh with the
    labor sweat of cablecar & Genoa papa pushcart

Bounty of electricity & visions carpented on pig-bastard
    night in its spore like the dim lights of some hallu-
    cinating facade

Ah tower from thy berryless head I'd a vision in com-
    mon with myself the proximity of Alcatraz and not
    the hip volley of white jazz & verse or verse & jazz
    embraced but a real heart-rending constant vision
    of Alcatraz marshaled before my eyes

Stocky Alcatraz weeping on Neptune's table whose
    petrific bondage crushes the dreamless seaharp

gasping for song O that that piece of sea fails to dream

Tower I'd a verdure vagueness fixed by a green wind the shade of Mercy lashed with cold nails against the wheatweather Western sky weeping I'm sure for humanity's vast door to open that all men be free that both hinge and lock die that all doors if they close close like Chinese bells

Was it man's love to screw the sky with monuments span the bay with orange & silver bridges shuttling structure into structure incorruptible in this endless tie each age impassions be it in stone or steel either in echo or halfheard ruin

Was it man's love that put that rock there never to avalanche but in vision or this imaginary now or myself standing on Telegraph Hill Nob Hill Russian Hill the same view always Alcatraz like a deserted holiday

And I cried for Alcatraz there in your dumb hollows O tower clenching my Pan's foot with vivid hoard of Dannemora

Cried for that which was no longer sovereign in me stinking of dead dreams dreams I yet feign to bury thus to shun reality's worm

Dreams that once jumped joyous bright from my heart

like sparks issued from a wild sharper's wheel now
     issued no longer
Were't not for cities or prisons O tower I might yet
     be that verdure monk lulling over green country
     albums with no greater dream than my youth's
     dream
Eyes of my hands! Queen Penthesileia and her tribe!
     Messenger stars Doctor Deformous back from his
     leprosy and woe! Thracian ships! Joyprints of
     pure air!

From TRANSFORMATION & ESCAPE

I reached heaven and it was syrupy.
It was oppressively sweet.
Croaking substances stuck to my knees.
Of all substances St. Michael was stickiest.
I grabbed him and pasted him on my head.
I found God a gigantic fly paper.
I stayed out of his way.
I walked where everything smelled of burnt chocolate.
Meanwhile St. Michael was busy with his sword
hacking away at my hair.
I found Dante standing naked in a blob of honey.
Bears were licking his thighs.
I snatched St. Michael's sword
and quartered myself in a great circular adhesive.
My torso fell upon an elastic equilibrium.
As though shot from a sling
my torso whizzed at God fly paper.
My legs sank into some unimaginable sog.
My head, though weighed with the weight of
        St. Michael,
did not fall.
Fine strands of multi-colored gum
suspended it there.
My spirit stopped by my snared torso.
I pulled! I yanked! Rolled it left to right!

It bruised! It softened! It could not free!
The struggle of an Eternity!
An Eternity of pulls! of yanks!
Went back to my head,
St. Michael had sucked dry my brainpan!
Skull!
My skull!
Only skull in heaven!
Went to my legs.

I AM 25

With a love a madness for Shelley
Chatterton   Rimbaud
and the needy-yap of my youth
        has gone from ear to ear:
    I HATE OLD POETMEN!
Especially old poetmen who retract
who consult other old poetmen
who speak their youth in whispers,
saying:—I did those then
        but that was then
        that was then—
O I would quiet old men
say to them:—I am your friend
        what you once were, thru me
        you'll be again—
Then at night in the confidence of their homes
rip out their apology-tongues
        and steal their poems.

GREGORY CORSO

POETS HITCHHIKING ON
THE HIGHWAY

Of course I tried to tell him
but he cranked his head
        without an excuse.
I told him the sky chases
        the sun
And he smiled and said:
        "What's the use."
I was feeling like a demon
        again
So I said: "But the ocean chases
        the fish."
This time he laughed
        and said: "Suppose the
                strawberry were
                        pushed into a mountain."
After that I knew the
        war was on—
So we fought:
He said: "The apple-cart like a
                        broomstick-angel
                snaps & splinters
                        old dutch shoes."
I said: "Lightning will strike the old oak
        and free the fumes!"

He said: "Mad street with no name."
I said: "Bald killer! Bald killer! Bald killer!"
He said, getting real mad,
        "Firestoves! Gas! Couch!"
I said, only smiling,
        "I know God would turn back his head
        if I sat quietly and thought."
We ended by melting away,
    hating the air!

AWAY ONE YEAR

I think of New York City lost in stars
forgotten as a bluehaired pet of childhood love—
Tonight the night is full;
the stealthy Mayor in his fine discipline
moves in proportion like a large jewel with furry feet;
he taps his long straight nose through the years of
    his term,
a ghost with worry-thoughts of city—
Beneath the Washington Square arch he feigns to forget
the new denunciations of the day.
This has never been the Mayor of my city,
occasionally stopping in a barren area
with magnificent foundations in his eyes.

I have not promised blessing upon leaving Gotham gate;
in lovelier cities I join my dreams in whose care I depend
though not once owning love to any city but the city of
    my heart.
New York City. It is fierce now; chariot-locked in the sky
like a stag scraping its back against mountains.
Fierce as a doleful vision, giving piteous grammercy.
In a dying cat's Egyptian eyes
the lovely mouse is a man of dreams, so my city:
dreamy solace of rivers and bridges brightly
    onionskinned in the night.

Down many urchin avenues
I see the days of my city bearding its face
its measure of skeleton clanking like a stove
the shell of Death come to navigate a city to
    the tomb.

AFTER READING "IN THE CLEARING"
For the author, Robert Frost

Old bard I like you more
    now that I know you're
    no Saturday Evening Post philosopher
Nay but such who plagiarizes God
Whose pen is a rod
    miracling all that is lovely old lovely bard

I would not like to think
    what's safe is safer done
    that it were an ill-planned link
    you and Washington
A poet can be a true friend
    upon which a politician could depend
Yet as history doth show
    out of power no poems grow
Such twinship ends up
    with the poet in the cup
Were you younger this were so
    but you are old old you are Rome
    the wisdom of time—and no crow
    maketh your snowy head its home

Poe is my only American poet, sir
And my homeland were Greece and England
Shelley is my ichor—Demeter is my mother
And of the living Ginsberg's metaphor
        is all I care to understand
You undoubtedly think unwell of us
But we are your natural children

WRIT ON THE EVE OF MY 32nd BIRTHDAY

a slow thoughtful spontaneous poem

I am 32 years old
and finally I look my age, if not more.
Is it a good face what's no more a boy's face?
It seems fatter. And my hair,
it's stopped being curly. Is my nose big?
The lips are the same.
And the eyes, ah the eyes get better all the time.
32 and no wife, no baby; no baby hurts,
        but there's lots of time.
I don't act silly any more.
And because of it I have to hear from so-called friends:
"You've changed. You used to be so crazy so great."
They are not comfortable with me when I'm serious.
Let them go to the Radio City Music Hall.
32; saw all of Europe, met millions of people;
        was great for some, terrible for others.
I remember my 31st year when I cried:
"To think I may have to go another 31 years!"
I don't feel that way this birthday.
I feel I want to be wise with white hair in a tall library
        in a deep chair by a fireplace.
Another year in which I stole nothing.
8 years now and haven't stole a thing!

I stopped stealing!
But I still lie at times,
and still am shameless yet ashamed when it comes
    to asking for money.
32 years old and four hard real funny sad bad
    wonderful books of poetry
—the world owes me a million dollars.

I think I had a pretty weird 32 years.
And it weren't up to me, none of it.
No choice of two roads; if there were,
    I don't doubt I'd have chosen both.
I like to think *chance* had it I play the bell.
The clue, perhaps, is in my unabashed declaration:
"I'm good example there's such a thing as called soul."
I love poetry because it makes me love
    and presents me life.
And of all the fires that die in me,
there's one burns like the sun;
it might not make day my personal life,
    my association with people,
      or my behavior toward society,
but it does tell me my soul has a shadow.

GREGORY CORSO   33

SECOND NIGHT IN N.Y.C. AFTER 3 YEARS

I was happy I was bubbly drunk
The street was dark
I waved to a young policeman
He smiled
I went up to him and like a flood of gold
Told him all about my prison youth
About how noble and great the convicts were
And about how I just returned from Europe
Which wasn't half as enlightening as prison
And he listened attentively I told no lie
Everything was truth and humor
He laughed
He laughed
And it made me so happy I said:
"Absolve it all, kiss me!"
"No no no no!" he said
      and hurried away.

"TRUST YOURSELF—BUT NOT TOO FAR"

"Trust yourself—but not too far"
El Paso fortune on the weighing machine
Sunday trolley/
       full of fleshly Mexicans going to
Mexico (Juarez) just over the
border—not me
"Gone to Mexico—gone home"
       Gone to
            Death
"Death"

       Joke—someone drops pointed paper
       cups (one by one—into the
       long plastic container—
       next to the watercooler
       in the office) and they are falling—
       slowly—and make no
       sound in my ears

CHASING THE BIRD

The sun sets unevenly and the people
go to bed.

The night has a thousand eyes.
The clouds are low, overhead.

Every night it is a little bit
more difficult, a little

harder. My mind
to me a mangle is.

THE DISHONEST MAILMEN

They are taking all my letters, and they
put them into a fire.

                       I see the flames, etc.
But do not care, etc.

They burn everything I have, or what little
I have. I don't care, etc.

The poem supreme, addressed to
emptiness—this is the courage

necessary. This is something
quite different.

I KNOW A MAN

As I sd to my
friend, because I am
always talking,—John, I

sd, which was not his
name, the darkness sur-
rounds us, what

can we do against
it, or else, shall we &
why not, buy a goddamn big car,

drive, he sd, for
christ's sake, look
out where yr going.

THE END

When I know what people think of me
I am plunged into my loneliness. The gray

hat bought earlier sickens.
I have no purpose no longer distinguishable.

A feeling like being choked
enters my throat.

THE HILL

It is some time since I have been
to what it was had once turned me
and made my head into
a cruel instrument.

It is simple
to confess. Then done,
to walk away, walk away,
to come again.

But that form, I must answer,
is dead in me, completely,
and I will not allow it
to reappear—

Saith perversity, the willful,
the magnanimous cruelty,
which is in me
like a hill.

THE RAIN

All night the sound had
come back again,
and again falls
this quiet, persistent rain.

What am I to myself
that must be remembered,
insisted upon
so often? Is it

that never the ease,
even the hardness,
of rain falling
will have for me

something other than this,
something not so insistent—
am I to be locked in this
final uneasiness.

Love, if you love me,
lie next to me.
Be for me, like rain,
the getting out

of the tiredness, the fatuousness, the semi-
lust of intentional indifference.
Be wet
with a decent happiness.

FOR LOVE
For Bobbie

Yesterday I wanted to
speak of it, that sense above
the others to me
important because all

that I know derives
from what it teaches me.
Today, what is it that
is finally so helpless,

different, despairs of its own
statement, wants to
turn away, endlessly
to turn away.

If the moon did not . . .
no, if you did not
I wouldn't either, but
what would I not

do, what prevention, what
thing so quickly stopped.
That is love yesterday
or tomorrow, not

now. Can I eat
what you give me. I
have not earned it. Must
I think of everything

as earned. Now love also
becomes a reward so
remote from me I have
only made it with my mind.

Here is tedium,
despair, a painful
sense of isolation and
whimsical if pompous

self-regard. But that image
is only of the mind's
vague structure, vague to me
because it is my own.

Love, what do I think
to say. I cannot say it.
What have you become to ask,
what have I made you into,

companion, good company,
crossed legs with skirt, or

soft body under
the bones of the bed.

Nothing says anything
but that which it wishes
would come true, fears
what else might happen in

some other place, some
other time not this one.
A voice in my place, an
echo of that only in yours.

Let me stumble into
not the confession but
the obsession I begin with
now. For you

also (also)
some time beyond place, or
place beyond time, no
mind left to

say anything at all,
that face gone, now.
Into the company of love
it all returns.

ROBERT CREELEY   45

REVOLUTIONARY LETTER #1

I have just realized that the stakes are myself
I have no other
ransom money, nothing to break or barter but my life
my spirit measured out, in bits, spread over
the roulette table, I recoup what I can
nothing else to shove under the nose of the *maître de jeu*
nothing to thrust out the window, no white flag
this flesh all I have to offer, to make the play with
this immediate head, what it comes up with, my move
as we slither over this go board, stepping always
(we hope) between the lines

POEM IN PRAISE OF MY HUSBAND
(TAOS)

I suppose it hasn't been easy living with me either,
with my piques, and ups and downs, my need
        for privacy
leo pride and weeping in bed when you're trying
        to sleep
and you, interrupting me in the middle of a
        thousand poems
did I call the insurance people? the time you stopped
        a poem
in the middle of our drive over the nebraska hills and
into colorado, odetta singing, the whole world
        singing in me
the triumph of our revolution in the air
me about to get that down, and you
you saying something about the carburetor
so that it all went away

but we cling to each other
as if each thought the other was the raft
and he adrift alone, as in this mud house
not big enough, the walls dusting down around us,
        a fine dust rain
counteracting the good, high air, and stuffing
        our nostrils

we hang our pictures of the several worlds:
new york collage, and san francisco posters,
set out our japanese dishes, chinese knives
hammer small indian marriage cloths into the adobe
we stumble thru silence into each other's gut
blundering thru from one wrong place to the next
like kids who snuck out to play on a boat at night
and the boat slipped from its moorings, and they look
     at the stars
about which they know nothing, to find out
where they are going

THE QUARREL

You know I said to Mark that I'm furious at you.

No he said are you bugged. He was drawing Brad who was asleep on the bed.

Yes I said I'm pretty god damned bugged. I sat down by the fire and stuck my feet out to warm them up.

Jesus I thought you think it's so easy. There you sit innocence personified. I didn't say anything else to him.

You know I thought I've got work to do too sometimes. In fact I probably have just as fucking much work to do as you do. A piece of wood fell out of the fire and I poked it back in with my toe.

I am sick I said to the woodpile of doing dishes. I am just as lazy as you. Maybe lazier. The toe of my shoe was scorched from the fire and I rubbed it where the suede was gone.

Just because I happen to be a chick I thought.

Mark finished one drawing and looked at it. Then he put it down and started another one.

It's damned arrogant of you I thought to assume that only you have things to do. Especially tonight.

And what a god damned concession it was for me to bother to tell you that I was bugged at all I said to the back of his neck. I didn't say it out loud.

I got up and went into the kitchen to do the dishes. And shit I thought I probably won't bother again. But I'll get bugged and not bother to tell you and after a while everything will be awful and I'll never say anything because it's so fucking uncool to talk about it. And that I thought will be that and what a shame.

Hey hon Mark yelled at me from the living room. It says here Picasso produces fourteen hours a day.

APRIL FOOL BIRTHDAY POEM
FOR GRANDPA

Today is your
birthday and I have tried
writing these things before,
but now
in the gathering madness, I want to
thank you
for telling me what to expect
for pulling
no punches, back there in that scrubbed Bronx parlor
thank you
for honestly weeping in time to
innumerable heartbreaking
italian operas for
pulling my hair when I
pulled the leaves off the trees so I'd
know how it feels, we are
involved in it now, revolution, up to our
knees and the tide is rising, I embrace
strangers on the street, filled with their love and
mine, the love you told us had to come or we
die, told them all in that Bronx park, me listening in
spring Bronx dusk, breathing stars, so glorious
to me your white hair, your height your fierce
blue eyes, rare among italians, I stood

a ways off, looking up at you, my grandpa
people listened to, I stand
a ways off listening as I pour out soup
young men with light in their faces
at my table, talking love, talking revolution
which is love, spelled backwards, how
you would love us all, would thunder your anarchist
        wisdom
at us, would thunder Dante, and Giordano Bruno,
        orderly men
bent to your ends, well I want you to know
we do it for you, and your ilk, for Carlo Tresca,
for Sacco and Vanzetti, without knowing
it, or thinking about it, as we do it for Aubrey
        Beardsley
Oscar Wilde (all street lights
shall be purple), do it
for Trotsky and Shelley and big/dumb
Kropotkin
Eisenstein's Strike people, Jean Cocteau's ennui,
        we do it for
the stars over the Bronx
that they may look on earth
and not be ashamed.

POETICS

I have deserted my post, I cdnt hold it
rearguard/to preserve the language/lucidity
let the language fend for itself.
it has turned over god knows enough carts in the
    city streets
its barricades are my nightmares

preserve the language!—there are
              enough fascists &
              enough socialists
on both sides
so that no one will lose this war

the language shall be my element, I plunge in
I suspect that I cannot drown
like a fat brat catfish, smug
              a hoodlum fish
I move more & more gracefully,
           breathe it in,
success written on my mug till the fishpolice
corner me in the coral & I die

#9

          "Truth is not the secret of a few"
                                        yet
you would maybe think so
                          the way some
          librarians
and cultural ambassadors and
                          especially museum directors
                                            act

          you'd think they had a corner
                                        on it
          the way they
                          walk around shaking
          their high heads and
                          looking as if they never
          went to the bath
                          room or anything

          But I wouldn't blame them
      if I were you
                    They say the Spiritual is best conceived
      in abstract terms
                    and then too
          walking around in museums always makes me

54

want to
       "sit down"
I always feel so
           constipated
in those
     high altitudes

#13

It was a face which darkness could kill
                              in an instant
    a face as easily hurt
                    by laughter or light
        "We *think* differently at night"
                            she told me once
lying back languidly

            And she would quote Cocteau

"I feel there is an angel in me" she'd say
                    "whom I am constantly shocking"

    Then she would smile and look away
            light a cigarette for me
                                sigh and rise
and stretch
            her sweet anatomy
                            let fall a stocking

#22

    crazy

        to be alive in such a strange
                        world

with the band playing schmaltz
                in the classic bandshell
                    and the people
  on the benches under the clipped trees
                  and girls
    on the grass
          and the breeze blowing and the
          streamers
    streaming
     and a fat man with a graflex
     and a dark woman with a dark dog she called
                    Lucia
     and a cat on a leash
     and a pekinese with a blond baby
     and a cuban in a fedora
     and a bunch of boys posing for a group
                  picture
and just then
    while the band went right on playing

                                        schmaltz
        a midget ran past shouting and waving his hat
                                        at someone
            and a young man with a gay campaignbutton
came up and said
                        Are you by any chance a registered
                                DEMOCRAT?

#39

A blockage in the bowel
       causes hang-ups in dreams
              or so it sometimes seems
as for instance when
      Sisyphus keeps trying all the time
         to roll that boulder up
        and it comes always rolling back
                 down upon him
or as when we cannot get across
            that symbolic railroad crossing
     where the train keeps bearing down on us
               all the time
     where you sit helpless at the helm
        of a wheelless
             Presidential limousine
    with fifty-one clowns in the back
    all wearing nothing but
          Stars & Stripes
    and all of them singing
            God Help America!

From HOWL
For Carl Solomon

I saw the best minds of my generation destroyed by
      madness, starving hysterical naked,
dragging themselves through the negro streets at dawn
      looking for an angry fix,
angelheaded hipsters burning for the ancient heavenly
      connection to the starry dynamo in the machinery
      of night,
who poverty and tatters and hollow-eyed and high sat
      up smoking in the supernatural darkness of cold-
      water flats floating across the tops of cities contem-
      plating jazz,
who bared their brains to Heaven under the El and
      saw Mohammedan angels staggering on tenement
      roofs illuminated,
who passed through universities with radiant cool eyes
      hallucinating Arkansas and Blake-light tragedy
      among the scholars of war,
who were expelled from the academies for crazy & pub-
      lishing obscene odes on the windows of the skull,
who cowered in unshaven rooms in underwear, burning
      their money in wastebaskets and listening to the
      Terror through the wall,
who got busted in their pubic beards returning through
      Laredo with a belt of marijuana for New York,

who ate fire in paint hotels or drank turpentine in
Paradise Alley, death, or purgatoried their torsos
night after night
with dreams, with drugs, with waking nightmares,
alcohol and cock and endless balls,
incomparable blind streets of shuddering cloud and
lightning in the mind leaping toward poles of
Canada & Paterson, illuminating all the motionless
world of Time between,
Peyote solidities of halls, backyard green tree cemetery
dawns, wine drunkenness over the rooftops, store-
front boroughs of teahead joyride neon blinking
traffic light, sun and moon and tree vibrations
in the roaring winter dusks of Brooklyn, ashcan
rantings and kind king light of mind,
who chained themselves to subways for the endless ride
from Battery to holy Bronx on benzedrine until
the noise of wheels and children brought them
down shuddering mouth-wracked and battered
bleak of brain all drained of brilliance in the drear
light of Zoo,
who sank all night in submarine light of Bickford's
floated out and sat through the stale beer afternoon
in desolate Fugazzi's, listening to the crack of
doom on the hydrogen jukebox,
who talked continuously seventy hours from park to
pad to bar to Bellevue to museum to the Brooklyn
Bridge,

61

a lost battalion of platonic conversationalists jumping
    down the stoops off fire escapes off windowsills off
    Empire State out of the moon,
yacketayakking screaming vomiting whispering facts
    and memories and anecdotes and eyeball kicks and
    shocks of hospitals and jails and wars,
whole intellects disgorged in total recall for seven days
    and nights with brilliant eyes, meat for the Syn-
    agogue cast on the pavement,
who vanished into nowhere Zen New Jersey leaving a
    trail of ambiguous picture postcards of Atlantic
    City Hall,
suffering Eastern sweats and Tangerian bone-
    grindings and migraines of China under junk-
    withdrawal in Newark's bleak furnished room,
who wandered around and around at midnight in the
    railroad yard wondering where to go, and went,
    leaving no broken hearts,
who lit cigarettes in boxcars boxcars boxcars racketing
    through snow toward lonesome farms in grand-
    father night,
who studied Plotinus Poe St. John of the Cross telepathy
    and bop kabbalah because the cosmos instinctively
    vibrated at their feet in Kansas,
who loned it through the streets of Idaho seeking
    visionary indian angels who were visionary indian
    angels,

62

who thought they were only mad when Baltimore
  gleamed in supernatural ecstasy,

who jumped in limousines with the Chinaman of Okla-
  homa on the impulse of winter midnight street-
  light smalltown rain,

who lounged hungry and lonesome through Houston
  seeking jazz or sex or soup, and followed the
  brilliant Spaniard to converse about America and
  Eternity, a hopeless task, and so took ship to Africa,

who disappeared into the volcanoes of Mexico leaving
  behind nothing but the shadow of dungarees and
  the lava and ash of poetry scattered in fireplace
  Chicago,

who reappeared on the West Coast investigating the
  F.B.I. in beards and shorts with big pacifist eyes
  sexy in their dark skin passing out incomprehen-
  sible leaflets,

who burned cigarette holes in their arms protesting the
  narcotic tobacco haze of Capitalism,

who distributed Supercommunist pamphlets in Union
  Square weeping and undressing while the sirens
  of Los Alamos wailed them down, and wailed down
  Wall, and the Staten Island ferry also wailed,

who broke down crying in white gymnasiums naked
  and trembling before the machinery of other
  skeletons,

who bit detectives in the neck and shrieked with delight

in policecars for committing no crime but their
own wild cooking pederasty and intoxication,

who howled on their knees in the subway and were
dragged off the roof waving genitals and
manuscripts,

who let themselves be fucked in the ass by saintly
motorcyclists, and screamed with joy,

who blew and were blown by those human seraphim,
the sailors, caresses of Atlantic and Caribbean love,

who balled in the morning in the evenings in rose-
gardens and the grass of public parks and cemeter-
ies scattering their semen freely to whomever
come who may,

who hiccuped endlessly trying to giggle but wound up
with a sob behind a partition in a Turkish Bath
when the blond & naked angel came to pierce them
with a sword,

who lost their loveboys to the three old shrews of fate
the one eyed shrew of the heterosexual dollar the
one eyed shrew that winks out of the womb and
the one eyed shrew that does nothing but sit on
her ass and snip the intellectual golden threads of
the craftsman's loom,

who copulated ecstatic and insatiate with a bottle of
beer a sweetheart a package of cigarettes a candle
and fell off the bed, and continued along the floor
and down the hall and ended fainting on the wall

with a vision of ultimate cunt and come eluding
the last gyzym of consciousness,

who sweetened the snatches of a million girls trembling
in the sunset, and were red eyed in the morning
but prepared to sweeten the snatch of the sunrise,
flashing buttocks under barns and naked in the
lake,

who went out whoring through Colorado in myriad
stolen night-cars, N.C., secret hero of these poems,
cocksman and Adonis of Denver—joy to the
memory of his innumerable lays of girls in empty
lots & diner backyards, moviehouses' rickety rows,
on mountaintops in caves or with gaunt waitresses
in familiar roadside lonely petticoat upliftings &
especially secret gas-station solipsisms of johns,
& hometown alleys too,

who faded out in vast sordid movies, were shifted in
dreams, woke on a sudden Manhattan, and picked
themselves up out of basements hungover with
heartless Tokay and horrors of Third Avenue iron
dreams & stumbled to unemployment offices,

who walked all night with their shoes full of blood on
the snowbank docks waiting for a door in the East
River to open to a room full of steamheat and
opium,

who created great suicidal dramas on the apartment
cliff-banks of the Hudson under the wartime blue

floodlight of the moon & their heads shall be crowned with laurel in oblivion,

who ate the lamb stew of the imagination or digested the crab at the muddy bottom of the rivers of Bowery,

who wept at the romance of the streets with their push-carts full of onions and bad music,

who sat in boxes breathing in the darkness under the bridge, and rose up to build harpsichords in their lofts,

who coughed on the sixth floor of Harlem crowned with flame under the tubercular sky surrounded by orange crates of theology,

who scribbled all night rocking and rolling over lofty incantations which in the yellow morning were stanzas of gibberish,

who cooked rotten animals lung heart feet tail borsht & tortillas dreaming of the pure vegetable kingdom,

who plunged themselves under meat trucks looking for an egg,

who threw their watches off the roof to cast their ballot for Eternity outside of Time, & alarm clocks fell on their heads every day for the next decade,

who cut their wrists three times successively unsuccess-fully, gave up and were forced to open antique stores where they thought they were growing old and cried,

who were burned alive in their innocent flannel suits

on Madison Avenue amid blasts of leaden verse
& the tanked-up clatter of the iron regiments of
fashion & the nitroglycerine shrieks of the fairies
of advertising & the mustard gas of sinister intelli-
gent editors, or were run down by the drunken
taxicabs of Absolute Reality,

who jumped off the Brooklyn Bridge this actually
happened and walked away unknown and forgot-
ten into the ghostly daze of Chinatown soup
alleyways & firetrucks, not even one free beer,

who sang out of their windows in despair, fell out of
the subway window, jumped in the filthy Passaic,
leaped on negroes, cried all over the street, danced
on broken wineglasses barefoot smashed phono-
graph records of nostalgic European 1930s
German jazz finished the whiskey and threw up
groaning into the bloody toilet, moans in their
ears and the blast of colossal steamwhistles,

who barreled down the highways of the past journeying
to each other's hotrod-Golgotha jail-solitude
watch or Birmingham jazz incarnation,

who drove crosscountry seventytwo hours to find out
if I had a vision or you had a vision or he had a
vision to find out Eternity,

who journeyed to Denver, who died in Denver, who
came back to Denver & waited in vain, who
watched over Denver & brooded & loned in Denver

and finally went away to find out the Time, & now
    Denver is lonesome for her heroes,

who fell on their knees in hopeless cathedrals praying
    for each other's salvation and light and breasts,
    until the soul illuminated its hair for a second,

who crashed through their minds in jail waiting for
    impossible criminals with golden heads and the
    charm of reality in their hearts who sang sweet
    blues to Alcatraz,

who retired to Mexico to cultivate a habit, or Rocky
    Mount to tender Buddha or Tangiers to boys
    or Southern Pacific to the black locomotive or
    Harvard to Narcissus to Woodlawn to the daisy-
    chain or grave,

who demanded sanity trials accusing the radio of
    hypnotism & were left with their insanity & their
    hands & a hung jury,

who threw potato salad at CCNY lecturers on Dadaism
    and subsequently presented themselves on the
    granite steps of the madhouse with shaven heads
    and harlequin speech of suicide, demanding
    instantaneous lobotomy,

and who were given instead the concrete void of insulin
    Metrazol electricity hydrotherapy psychotherapy
    occupational therapy pingpong & amnesia,

who in humorless protest overturned only one symbolic
    pingpong table, resting briefly in catatonia,

returning years later truly bald except for a wig of
blood, and tears and fingers, to the visible madman
doom of the wards of the madtowns of the East,
Pilgrim State's Rockland's and Greystone's foetid halls,
bickering with the echoes of the soul, rocking and
rolling in the midnight solitude-bench dolmen-
realms of love, dream of life a nightmare, bodies
turned to stone as heavy as the moon,
with mother finally ******, and the last fantastic book
flung out of the tenement window, and the last
door closed at 4 A.M. and the last telephone
slammed at the wall in reply and the last furnished
room emptied down to the last piece of mental
furniture, a yellow paper rose twisted on a wire
hanger in the closet, and even that imaginary,
nothing but a hopeful little bit of hallucination—
ah, Carl, while you are not safe I am not safe, and now
you're really in the total animal soup of time—
and who therefore ran through the icy streets obsessed
with a sudden flash of the alchemy of the use of the
ellipse the catalog the meter & the vibrating plane,
who dreamt and made incarnate gaps in Time & Space
through images juxtaposed, and trapped the arch-
angel of the soul between 2 visual images and
joined the elemental verbs and set the noun and
dash of consciousness together jumping with
sensation of Pater Omnipotens Aeterna Deus

to recreate the syntax and measure of poor human prose
and stand before you speechless and intelligent
and shaking with shame, rejected yet confessing
out the soul to conform to the rhythm of thought
in his naked and endless head,

the madman bum and angel beat in Time, unknown yet
putting down here what might be left to say in
time come after death,

and rose reincarnate in the ghostly clothes of jazz in
the goldhorn shadow of the band and blew the
suffering of America's naked mind for love into an
eli eli lamma lamma sabacthani saxophone cry that
shivered the cities down to the last radio

with the absolute heart of the poem of life butchered out
of their own bodies good to eat a thousand years.

"BACK ON TIMES SQUARE, DREAMING OF TIMES SQUARE"

Let some sad trumpeter stand
   on the empty streets at dawn
and blow a silver chorus to the
   buildings of Times Square,
memorial of ten years, at 5 A.M., with
   the thin white moon just
     visible
  above the green & grooking McGraw
   Hill offices
a cop walks by, but he's invisible
   with his music

The Globe Hotel, Garver lay in
   grey beds there and hunched his
   back and cleaned his needles—
where I lay many nights on the nod
   from his leftover bloody cottons
   and dreamed of Blake's voice talking—
     I was lonely,
    Garver's dead in Mexico two years,
   hotel's vanished into a parking lot
And I'm back here—sitting on the streets
again—

The movies took our language, the
great red signs
A DOUBLE BILL OF GASSERS
Teen Age Nightmare
Hooligans of the Moon

But we were never nightmare
hooligans but seekers of
the blond nose for Truth

Some old men are still alive, but
the old Junkies are gone—

We are a legend, invisible but
legendary, as prophesied

MY ALBA

Now that I've wasted
five years in Manhattan
life decaying
talent a blank

talking disconnected
patient and mental
sliderule and number
machine on a desk

autographed triplicate
synopsis and taxes
obedient prompt
poorly paid

stayed on the market
youth of my twenties
fainted in offices
wept on typewriters

deceived multitudes
in vast conspiracies
deodorant battleships
serious business industry

every six weeks whoever
drank my blood bank
innocent evil now
part of my system

five years unhappy labor
22 to 27 working
not a dime in the bank
to show for it anyway

dawn breaks it's only the sun
the East smokes O my bedroom
I am damned to Hell what
alarmclock is ringing

SONG

The weight of the world
　　　is love.
Under the burden
　　　of solitude,
under the burden
　　　of dissatisfaction

　　　the weight,
the weight we carry
　　　is love.

Who can deny?
　　　In dreams
it touches
　　　the body,
in thought
　　　constructs
a miracle,
　　　in imagination
anguishes
　　　till born
in human—

looks out of the heart
　　　burning with purity—
for the burden of life
　　　is love,

but we carry the weight
        wearily,
and so must rest
in the arms of love
        at last,
must rest in the arms
        of love.

No rest
        without love,
no sleep
        without dreams
of love—
        be mad or chill
obsessed with angels
        or machines,
the final wish
        is love
—cannot be bitter,
        cannot deny,
cannot withhold
        if denied:

the weight is too heavy

        —must give
for no return
        as thought

is given
        in solitude
in all the excellence
        of its excess.

The warm bodies
        shine together
in the darkness,
        the hand moves
to the center
        of the flesh,
the skin trembles
        in happiness
and the soul comes
        joyful to the eye—

yes, yes,
        that's what
I wanted,
        I always wanted,
I always wanted,
        to return
to the body
        where I was born.

ALLEN GINSBERG   77

MALEST CORNIFICI TUO CATULLO

I'm happy, Kerouac, your madman Allen's
finally made it: discovered a new young cat,
and my imagination of an eternal boy
walks on the streets of San Francisco,
handsome, and meets me in cafeterias
and loves me. Ah don't think I'm sickening.
You're angry at me. For all of my lovers?
It's hard to eat shit, without having visions;
when they have eyes for me it's like Heaven.

TEARS

I'm crying all the time now.
I cried all over the street when I left the Seattle
    Wobbly Hall.
I cried listening to Bach.
I cried looking at the happy flowers in my backyard,
    I cried at the sadness of the middle-aged trees.

Happiness exists I feel it.
I cried for my soul, I cried for the world's soul.
The world has a beautiful soul.
God appearing to be seen and cried over. Overflowing
    heart of Paterson.

From KADDISH

For Naomi Ginsberg 1894–1956

Strange now to think of you, gone without corsets &
    eyes, while I walk on the sunny pavement of
    Greenwich Village.

downtown Manhattan, clear winter noon, and I've been
    up all night, talking, talking, reading the Kaddish
    aloud, listening to Ray Charles blues shout blind
    on the phonograph

the rhythm the rhythm—and your memory in my head
    three years after—And read Adonais' last trium-
    phant stanzas aloud—wept, realizing how we
    suffer—

And how Death is that remedy all singers dream of,
    sing, remember, prophesy as in the Hebrew
    Anthem, or the Buddhist Book of Answers—and
    my own imagination of a withered leaf—at dawn—

Dreaming back thru life, Your time—and mine acceler-
    ating toward Apocalypse,

the final moment—the flower burning in the Day—and
    what comes after,

looking back on the mind itself that saw an American
    city

a flash away, and the great dream of Me or China, or
    you and a phantom Russia, or a crumpled bed that
    never existed—

like a poem in the dark—escaped back to Oblivion—

No more to say, and nothing to weep for but the Beings in the Dream, trapped in its disappearance,

sighing, screaming with it, buying and selling pieces of phantom, worshiping each other,

worshiping the God included in it all—longing or inevitability?—while it lasts, a Vision—anything more?

It leaps about me, as I go out and walk the street, look back over my shoulder, Seventh Avenue, the battlements of window office buildings shouldering each other high, under a cloud, tall as the sky an instant—and the sky above—an old blue place.

or down the Avenue to the South, to—as I walk toward the Lower East Side—where you walked 50 years ago, little girl—from Russia, eating the first poisonous tomatoes of America—frightened on the dock—

then struggling in the crowds of Orchard Street toward what?—toward Newark—

toward candy store, first home-made sodas of the century, hand-churned ice cream in backroom on musty brownfloor boards—

Toward education marriage nervous breakdown, opera-

tion, teaching school, and learning to be mad, in a
   dream—what is this life?
Toward the Key in the window—and the great Key
   lays its head of light on top of Manhattan, and over
   the floor, and lays down on the sidewalk—in a
   single vast beam, moving, as I walk down First
   toward the Yiddish Theater—and the place of
   poverty
you knew, and I know, but without caring now—
   Strange to have moved thru Paterson, and the
   West, and Europe and here again,
with the cries of Spaniards now in the doorstoops doors
   and dark boys on the street, fire escapes old as you
—Tho you're not old now, that's left here with me—
Myself, anyhow, maybe as old as the universe—and
   I guess that dies with us—enough to cancel all
   that comes—What came is gone forever every
   time—
That's good! That leaves it open for no regret —no fear
   radiators, lacklove, torture even toothache in the
   end—
Though while it comes it is a lion that eats the soul—
   and the lamb, the soul, in us, alas, offering itself
   in sacrifice to change's fierce hunger—hair and
   teeth—and the roar of bonepain, skull bare, break
   rib, rot-skin, braintricked Implacability.
Ai! ai! we do worse! We are in a fix! And you're out,

Death let you out, Death had the Mercy, you're done with your century, done with God, done with the path thru it—Done with yourself at last—Pure—Back to the Babe dark before your Father, before us all—before the world—

There, rest. No more suffering for you. I know where you've gone, it's good.

A SUPERMARKET IN CALIFORNIA

What thoughts I have of you tonight, Walt Whitman,
for I walked down the sidestreets under the trees with
a headache self-conscious looking at the full moon.

In my hungry fatigue, and shopping for images, I
went into the neon fruit supermarket, dreaming of your
enumerations!

What peaches and what penumbras! Whole families
shopping at night! Aisles full of husbands! Wives in
the avocados, babies in the tomatoes!—and you, García
Lorca, what were you doing down by the watermelons?

I saw you, Walt Whitman, childless, lonely old
grubber, poking among the meats in the refrigerator
and eyeing the grocery boys.

I heard you asking questions of each: Who killed the
pork chops? What price bananas? Are you my Angel?

I wandered in and out of the brilliant stacks of cans
following you, and followed in my imagination by the
store detective.

We strode down the open corridors together in our
solitary fancy tasting artichokes, possessing every
frozen delicacy, and never passing the cashier.

Where are we going, Walt Whitman? The doors
close in an hour. Which way does your beard point
tonight?

(I touch your book and dream of our odyssey in the supermarket and feel absurd.)

Will we walk all night through solitary streets? The trees add shade to shade, lights out in the houses, we'll both be lonely.

Will we stroll dreaming of the lost America of love past blue automobiles in driveways, home to our silent cottage?

Ah, dear father, graybeard, lonely old courage-teacher, what America did you have when Charon quit poling his ferry and you got out on a smoking bank and stood watching the boat disappear on the black waters of Lethe?

SUNFLOWER SUTRA

I walked on the banks of the tincan banana dock and sat
    down under the huge shade of a Southern Pacific
    locomotive to look at the sunset over the box house
    hills and cry.
Jack Kerouac sat beside me on a busted rusty iron pole,
    companion, we thought the same thoughts of the
    soul, bleak and blue and sad-eyed, surrounded by
    the gnarled steel roots of trees of machinery.
The oily water on the river mirrored the red sky, sun
    sank on top of final Frisco peaks, no fish in that
    stream, no hermit in those mounts, just ourselves
    rheumy-eyed and hungover like old bums on the
    riverbank, tired and wily.
Look at the Sunflower, he said, there was a dead gray
    shadow against the sky, big as a man, sitting dry
    on top of a pile of ancient sawdust—
—I rushed up enchanted—it was my first sunflower,
    memories of Blake—my visions—Harlem
and Hells of the Eastern rivers, bridges clanking Joes
    Greasy Sandwiches, dead baby carriages, black
    treadless tires forgotten and unretreaded, the
    poem of the riverbank, condoms & pots, steel
    knives, nothing stainless, only the dank muck and
    the razor-sharp artifacts passing into the past—
and the gray Sunflower poised against the sunset,

crackly bleak and dusty with the smut and smog and
    smoke of olden locomotives in its eye—
corolla of bleary spikes pushed down and broken like a
    battered crown, seeds fallen out of its face, soon-
    to-be-toothless mouth of sunny air, sunrays
    obliterated on its hairy head like a dried wire
    spiderweb,
leaves stuck out like arms out of the stem, gestures from
    the sawdust root, broke pieces of plaster fallen out
    of the black twigs, a dead fly in its ear,
Unholy battered old thing you were, my sunflower O
    my soul, I loved you then!
The grime was no man's grime but death and human
    locomotives,
all that dress of dust, that veil of darkened railroad skin,
    that smog of cheek, that eyelid of black mis'ry, that
    sooty hand or phallus or protuberance of artificial
    worse-than-dirt—industrial—modern—all that
    civilization spotting your crazy golden crown—
and those blear thoughts of death and dusty loveless
    eyes and ends and withered roots below, in the
    home-pile of sand and sawdust, rubber dollar bills,
    skin of machinery, the guts and innards of the
    weeping coughing car, the empty lonely tincans
    with their rusty tongues alack, what more could

I name, the smoked ashes of some cock cigar, the cunts of wheelbarrows and the milky breasts of cars, wornout asses out of chairs & sphincters of dynamos—all these

entangled in your mummied roots—and you there standing before me in the sunset, all your glory in your form!

A perfect beauty of a sunflower! a perfect excellent lovely sunflower existence! a sweet natural eye to the new hip moon, woke up alive and excited grasping in the sunset shadow sunrise golden monthly breeze!

How many flies buzzed round you innocent of your grime, while you cursed the heavens of the railroad and your flower soul?

Poor dead flower? when did you forget you were a flower? when did you look at your skin and decide you were an impotent dirty old locomotive? the ghost of a locomotive? the specter and shade of a once powerful mad American locomotive?

You were never no locomotive, Sunflower, you were a sunflower!

And you Locomotive, you are a locomotive, forget me not!

So I grabbed up the skeleton thick sunflower and stuck it at my side like a scepter,

and deliver my sermon to my soul, and Jack's soul too,
   and anyone who'll listen,
—We're not our skin of grime, we're not our dread
   bleak dusty imageless locomotive, we're all beauti-
   ful golden sunflowers inside, we're blessed by our
   own seed & golden hairy naked accomplishment-
   bodies growing into mad black formal sunflowers
   in the sunset, spied on by our eyes under the
   shadow of the mad locomotive riverbank sunset
   Frisco hilly tincan evening sitdown vision.

From AMERICA

America I've given you all and now I'm nothing.
America two dollars and twentyseven cents
    January 17, 1956.
I can't stand my own mind.
America when will we end the human war?
Go fuck yourself with your atom bomb.
I don't feel good don't bother me.
I won't write my poem till I'm in my right mind.
America when will you be angelic?
When will you take off your clothes?
When will you look at yourself through the grave?
When will you be worthy of your million Trotskyites?
America why are your libraries full of tears?
America when will you send your eggs to India?
I'm sick of your insane demands.
When can I go into the supermarket and buy what
    I need with my good looks?
America after all it is you and I who are perfect not the
    next world.
Your machinery is too much for me.
You made me want to be a saint.
There must be some other way to settle this
    argument.
Burroughs is in Tangiers I don't think he'll come back
    it's sinister.

Are you being sinister or is this some form of
    practical joke?
I'm trying to come to the point.
I refuse to give up my obsession.
America stop pushing I know what I'm doing.
America the plum blossoms are falling.
I haven't read the newspapers for months, everyday
    somebody goes on trial for murder.
America I feel sentimental about the Wobblies.
America I used to be a communist when I was a kid
    I'm not sorry.
I smoke marijuana every chance I get.
I sit in my house for days on end and stare at the
    roses in the closet.
When I go to Chinatown I get drunk and never
    get laid.
My mind is made up there's going to be trouble.
You should have seen me reading Marx.
My psychoanalyst thinks I'm perfectly right.
I won't say the Lord's Prayer.
I have mystical visions and cosmic vibrations.
America I still haven't told you what you did to Uncle
    Max after he came over from Russia.

I'm addressing you.
Are you going to let your emotional life be run by
 Time Magazine?
I'm obsessed by Time Magazine.
I read it every week.
Its cover stares at me every time I slink past the corner
 candystore.
I read it in the basement of the Berkeley Public Library.
It's always telling me about responsibility.
 Businessmen are serious. Movie producers are
 serious. Everybody's serious but me.
It occurs to me that I am America.
I am talking to myself again.

PARACHUTES, MY LOVE, COULD CARRY US HIGHER

I just said I didn't know
And now you are holding me
In your arms,
How kind.
Parachutes, my love, could carry us higher.
Yet around the net I am floating
Pink and pale blue fish are caught in it,
They are beautiful,
But they are not good for eating.
Parachutes, my love, could carry us higher
Than this mid-air in which we tremble,
Having exercised our arms in swimming,
Now the suspension, you say,
Is exquisite. I do not know.
There is coral below the surface,
There is sand, and berries
Like pomegranates grow.
This wide net, I am treading water
Near it, bubbles are rising and salt
Drying on my lashes, yet I am no nearer
Air than water. I am closer to you
Than land and I am in a stranger ocean
Than I wished.

SUNDAY EVENING

I am telling you a number of half-conditioned ideas
Am repeating myself,
The room has four sides; it is a rectangle,
From the window the bridge, the water, the leaves,
Her hat is made of feathers,
My fortune is produced from glass
And I drink to my extinction.

Barges on the river carry apples wrapped in bales,
This morning there was a somber sunrise,
In the red, in the air, in what is falling through us
We quote several things.

I am talking to you
With what is left of me written off,
On the cuff, ancestral and vague,
As a monkey walks through the many fires
Of a jungle while a village breathes in its sleep.

Someone stops in the alcove,
It is a risk we will later make,
While I talk and you bring your eyes to the fiber
(as the blade to the brown root)
And the room is slumberous and slow
(as a pulse after the first September earthquake).

PREFACE TO A TWENTY VOLUME SUICIDE NOTE

For Kellie Jones, born 16 May 1959

Lately, I've become accustomed to the way
The ground opens up and envelops me
Each time I go out to walk the dog.
Or the broad edged silly music the wind
Makes when I run for a bus...

Things have come to that.

And now, each night I count the stars,
And each night I get the same number.
And when they will not come to be counted,
I count the holes they leave.

Nobody sings anymore.

And then last night, I tiptoed up
To my daughter's room and heard her
Talking to someone, and when I opened
The door, there was no one there...
Only she on her knees, peeking into

Her own clasped hands.

LEROI JONES

SEX, LIKE DESIRE

               (away from the streets. Flash
into pockets, the fingers' smell, deeply secret.
Each night, another rape. Young boys hide at the tops
of hills, near gas stations and breweries, waiting
to make the hit. It is not even love. Still, they
wait, and make believe

                     they are beautiful.

It could be me, even now. (So slow, I come to see
myself. To be at a point rusted in my dead child's
breast. Where the life is, all the flesh, to make
more than a silhouette, a breathless shadow counting
again, his change.

What is there? Where is it? Who is she? What can I
give myself, trade myself, to make me understand
myself? Nothing is ever finished. Nothing past. Each
act of my life, with me now, till death. Themselves,
the reasons for it. They are stones, in my mouth
and ears. Whole forests on my shoulders.

WAR POEM

The battle waxed (battle wax, good night!
        Steep tumors of the sea's energy
        shells, shells, gold lights under the tree's
        cover.)

        In spring the days explode
        In spain old cuckolds watch their wives
        and send their money to America.

        Straw roofs, birds, any thing we have not
        got. Destroyed before it got here. *Battle*,
        an old dead flower she put on her breast.

        Shells crush the beach. Are crushed
        beneath her feet. Wait for night,
        and the one soldier will not mind us
        sitting here, listening to the familiar
        water, scatter in the shadows.

POLITICAL POEM
For Basil

Luxury, then, is a way of
being ignorant, comfortably.
An approach to the open market
of least information. Where theories
can thrive, under heavy tarpaulins
without being cracked by ideas.

(I have not seen the earth for years
and think now possibly "dirt" is
negative, positive, but clearly
social. I cannot plant a seed, cannot
recognize the root with clearer dent
than indifference. Though I eat
and shit as a natural man. (Getting up
from the desk to secure a turkey sandwich
and answer the phone: the poem undone
undone by my station, by my station,
and the bad words of Newark.) Raised up
to the breech, we seek to fill for this
crumbling century. The darkness of love,
in whose sweating memory all error is forced.

Undone by the logic of any specific death.
        (Old gentlemen
who still follow fires, tho are quieter
and less punctual. It is a polite truth
we are left with. Who are you? What are you
saying? Something to be dealt with, as easily.
The noxious game of reason, saying, "No, No,
you cannot feel," like my dead lecturer
lamenting thru gipsies his fast suicide.

ENLIGHTENMENT POEM

we have all been brothers, hermaphroditic as oysters
bestowing our pearls carelessly

no one yet had invented ownership
nor guilt   nor time

we watched the seasons pass, we were as crystalline
      as snow
and melted gently into newer forms
as stars spun round our heads

we had not learned betrayal

our selves were pearls
irritants transmuted into luster
and offered   carelessly

our pearls became more precious and our sexes static
mutability grew a shell, we devised different languages
new words for new concepts, we invented alarm clocks
fences   loyalty

still . . . even now . . . making a feint at communion
      infinite perceptions
I remember
we have all been brothers
and offer   carelessly

BLUES FOR SISTER SALLY

I

moon-faced baby with cocaine arms
        nineteen summers
        nineteen lovers

  novice of the junkie angel
lay sister of mankind penitent
        sister in marijuana
        sister in hashish
        sister in morphine

against the bathroom grimy sink
pumping her arms full of life
        (holy holy)
she bears the stigma (holy holy) of the raving christ
        (holy holy)
        holy needle
        holy powder
        holy vein

dear miss lovelorn: my sister makes it with a hunk
of glass do you think this is normal miss lovelorn

I DEMAND AN ANSWER!

II

weep
for my sister she walks with open veins
leaving her blood in the sewers of your cities
                from east coast
                to west coast
                to nowhere

  how shall we canonize our sister who is not
      quite dead
          who fornicates with strangers
          who masturbates with needles
who is afraid of the dark and wears her long hair soft
      and black
          against her bloodless face

III

midnight and the room dream-green and hazy
we are all part of the collage

            brother and sister, she leans against the wall
            and he, slipping the needle in her painless arm

            pale fingers (with love) against the pale arm

IV

children our afternoon is soft, we lean against
   each other

         our stash is in our elbows
         our fix is in our heads
god is a junkie and he has sold salvation
      for a week's supply

JUNK/ANGEL

I have seen the junkie angel winging his devious path
    over cities
his greenblack pinions parting the air with the sound
    of fog
I have seen him plummet to earth, folding
his feathered bat wings against his narrow flesh
pausing to share the orisons of some ecstatic acolyte
The bone shines through his face
and he exudes the rainbow odor of corruption
his eyes are spirals of green radioactive mist
luminous even in sunlight   even at noon
his footstep is precise, his glance is tender
he has no mouth nor any other feature
but whirling eyes above the glaring faceless face
he never speaks and always understands he answers
    no one
Radiant with a black green radiance
he extends his hollow fingered hands
blessing   blessing   blessing
his ichorous hollow fingers caressing the shadow
    of the man
with love and avarice
and Then unfurls his wings and rides the sky like an
enormous Christian bat   and voiceless
flies behind the sun

BENEDICTION

Pale brown Moses went down to Egypt land
To let somebody's people go.
Keep him out of Florida, no UN there:
The poor governor is all alone,
With six hundred thousand illiterates.

America, I forgive you . . . I forgive you
Nailing black Jesus to an imported cross
Every six weeks in Dawson, Georgia.
America, I forgive you . . . I forgive you
Eating black children, I know your hunger.
America, I forgive you . . . I forgive you
Burning Japanese babies defensively—
I realize how necessary it was.
Your ancestor had beautiful thoughts in his brain.
His descendants are experts in real estate.
Your generals have mushrooming visions.
Every day your people get more and more
Cars, televisions, sickness, death dreams.
You must have been great
Alive.

WEST COAST SOUNDS—1956

San Fran, hipster land,
Jazz sounds, wig sounds,
Earthquake sounds, others,
Allen on Chestnut Street,
Giving poetry to squares,
Corso on knees, pleading,
God eyes.
Rexroth, Ferlinghetti,
Swinging, in cellars,
Kerouac at Locke's,
Writing Neil
On high typewriter,
Neil, booting a choo-choo,
On zigzag tracks.
Now, many cats
Falling in,
New York cats,
Too many cats,
Monterey scene cooler,
San Franers, falling down.
Canneries closing.
Sardines splitting
For Mexico.
Me too.

FRAGMENT

... All those dead movie stars, peanut-buttered forever,
Do they kiss famous horses on the nose?
Do they see all of the latest horror movies?
How do they like the exclusive tombs, renaissance
     mailboxes,
With Bela Lugosi moving around down there
In his capeman Agron suit, sleepless walker,
With his arms full of morphine, his eyes suggesting
Frozen seesaws in cold playgrounds of yesterday.
What came first? The chicken or the spike?
What came last? The needle or the haystack?
That scream was a rumor and remained unscreamed,
Unnoted among narcotic breakfasts and raving
     love fiends,
Sexy rides on Gothic streetcars and Buddha lost in
     a phone booth,
Cold talking wind-people, three-dimensional
     valentines,
Torn from magic tenements in the long Decembers
     of today.
Easter-faced skylarks, low-flying Mexican birds,
The oracle of the crickets ticking off jazz *Te Deums*,
Our Lady of Nicotine, madonna without child,
Releases her pale balloon, snatched from the
     folding year,

All the daring young headhunters, traumatic in
    inflammatory bathing suits,
Shriek grim fairy tales, while convenient needles fall
    out of haystacks.
Charlie Parker was a great electrician who went
    around wiring people.

GINSBERG
For Allen

Ginsberg won't stop tossing lions to the martyrs.
This ends the campaign by leftwing cardinals to elect
      an Eskimo Pope.
The Church is becoming alarmed by the number of
      people defecting to God.
The Holy Intelligence Agency is puzzled: they have
      proof he is broke and his agents
Use spiritual brainwashing in addition to promises of
      quick sainthood.
The holy stepfather cautioned the faithful to emulate
      none of the saints who hide behind the Fifth
      Commandment when persecuted.
There is also a move to cut off Ginsberg's supply of lions.
The poet continues to smoke carnal knowledge
      knowingly.
I am sure the government can't prove that he is stolen
      property;
I have proof that he was Gertrude Stein's medicine chest.
I am not not an I, secret wick, I do nothing, light
      myself, burn.
Allen passed through that Black Hole of Calcutta
      behind my eyes;
He was wearing rings and hoops of longitude and
      latitude.

He must have been hurt by real love, and false love, too.
He can cling and fall and clasp eyes with the best,
Design exciting families with no people in them,
Stuffed with bleeding expressions of human form.
Why I love him, though, is equatorially sound:
I love him because his eyes leak.

ABOMUNIST MANIFESTO

ABOMUNISTS JOIN NOTHING BUT THEIR HANDS OR LEGS,
OR OTHER SAME.

ABOMUNISTS SPIT ANTI-POETRY FOR POETIC REASONS
AND FRINK.

ABOMUNISTS DO NOT LOOK AT PICTURES PAINTED BY
PRESIDENTS AND UNEMPLOYED PRIME MINISTERS.

IN TIMES OF NATIONAL PERIL, ABOMUNISTS, AS REALITY
AMERICANS, STAND READY TO DRINK THEMSELVES
TO DEATH FOR THEIR COUNTRY.

ABOMUNISTS DO NOT FEEL PAIN, NO MATTER HOW MUCH
IT HURTS.

ABOMUNISTS DO NOT USE THE WORD SQUARE EXCEPT
WHEN TALKING TO SQUARES.

ABOMUNISTS READ NEWSPAPERS ONLY TO ASCERTAIN
THEIR ABOMINUBILITY.

ABOMUNISTS NEVER CARRY MORE THAN FIFTY DOLLARS
IN DEBTS ON THEM.

ABOMUNISTS BELIEVE THAT THE SOLUTION OF PROBLEMS
OF RELIGIOUS BIGOTRY IS, TO HAVE A CATHOLIC
CANDIDATE FOR PRESIDENT AND A PROTESTANT
CANDIDATE FOR POPE.

ABOMUNISTS DO NOT WRITE FOR MONEY; THEY WRITE
THE MONEY ITSELF.

ABOMUNISTS BELIEVE ONLY WHAT THEY DREAM ONLY
AFTER IT COMES TRUE.

ABOMUNIST CHILDREN MUST BE REARED ABOMUNIBLY.

ABOMUNIST POETS, CONFIDENT THAT THE NEW LITERARY
FORM "FOOT-PRINTISM" HAS FREED THE ARTIST OF
OUTMODED RESTRICTIONS, SUCH AS: THE ABILITY TO
READ AND WRITE, OR THE DESIRE TO COMMUNICATE,
MUST BE PREPARED TO READ THEIR WORK AT
DENTAL COLLEGES, EMBALMING SCHOOLS, HOMES FOR
UNWED MOTHERS, HOMES FOR WED MOTHERS,
INSANE ASYLUMS, USO CANTEENS, KINDERGARTENS,
AND COUNTY JAILS. ABOMUNISTS NEVER
COMPROMISE THEIR REJECTIONARY PHILOSOPHY.

ABOMUNISTS REJECT EVERYTHING EXCEPT SNOWMEN.

MEXICAN LONELINESS

And I am an unhappy stranger
grooking in the streets of Mexico—
My friends have died on me, my
lovers disappeared, my whores banned,
my bed rocked and heaved by
earthquake—and no holy weed
    to get high by candlelight
    and dream—only fumes of buses,
dust storms, and maids peeking at me
    thru a hole in the door
    secretly drilled to watch
    masturbators fuck pillows—
    I am the Gargoyle
    of Our Lady
        dreaming in space
        gray mist dreams—
My face is pointed towards Napoleon
——I have no form——
My address book is full of RIP's
    I have no value in the void,
        at home without honor,—
My only friend is an old fag
        without a typewriter
Who, if he's my friend,
        I'll be buggered.

I have some mayonnaise left,
a whole unwanted bottle of oil,
peasants washing my sky light,
   a nut clearing his throat
   in the bathroom next to mine
   a hundred times a day
   sharing my common ceiling—
If I get drunk I get thirsty
—if I walk my foot breaks down
—if I smile my mask's a farce
—if I cry I'm just a child—
—if I remember I'm a liar
—if I write the writing's done—
—if I die the dying's over—
—if I live the dying's just begun—
—if I wait the waiting's longer
—if I go the going's gone—
if I sleep the bliss is heavy—
the bliss is heavy on my lids—
—if I go to cheap movies
    the bedbugs get me—
Expensive movies I can't afford
—If I do nothing
    nothing does

HOW TO MEDITATE

—lights out—
fall, hands a-clasped, into instantaneous
ecstasy like a shot of heroin or morphine,
the gland inside of my brain discharging
the good glad fluid (Holy Fluid) as
I hap-down and hold all my body parts
down to a deadstop trance—Healing
all my sicknesses—erasing all—not
even the shred of a "I-hope-you" or a
Loony Balloon left in it, but the mind
blank, serene, thoughtless. When a thought
comes a-springing from afar with its held-
forth figure of image, you spoof it out,
you spuff it off, you fake it, and
it fades, and thought never comes—and
with joy you realize for the first time
"Thinking's just like not thinking—
So I dont have to think
        any
      more"

JACK KEROUAC   115

A SUDDEN SKETCH POEM

Gary's sink has a shroudy burlap
   the rub brush tinware plout
    leans on right side
    like a red woman's hair
   the faucet leaks little lovedrops
The teacup's upsidedown with visions
     of green mountains and brown lousy
    Chinese mysterious up heights
   The frying pan's still wet
   The spoon's by 2 petals of flower
   The washrag's hung on edge like bloomers
   I dont know what to say
     about the dishpan, the soap
   The sink itself inside or what
   is hidden underneath the bomb burlap
Shroudflap except two onions
   And an orange and old wheat germ.
Wheat meal. The hoodlatch heliograph
With the cross that makes the devil
Hiss, ah, the upper coral sensen soups
   And fast condiments, curries, rices,
Roaches, reels, tin, tip, plastickets,
   Toothbrushes and armies, and armies
Of insulated schiller, squozen gumbrop

Peste pans, light of marin, pirshyar,
Magic dancing lights of gray and white
And all for verse I wrote it

HYMN

And when you showed me Brooklyn Bridge
  in the morning,
    Ah God,

And the people slipping on ice in the street,
twice,
     twice,
         two different people
         came over, goin to work,
         so earnest and tryful,
         clutching their pitiful
         morning Daily News
         slip on the ice & fall
         both inside 5 minutes
         and I cried I cried

That's when you taught me tears, Ah
  God in the morning,
    Ah Thee

And me leaning on the lamppost wiping
eyes,
     eyes,
         nobody's know I'd cried
         or woulda cared anyway

but O I saw my father
and my grandfather's mother
and the long lines of chairs
and tear-sitters and dead,
Ah me, I knew God You
had better plans than that

So whatever plan you have for me
Splitter of majesty
Make it short
    brief
Make it snappy
    bring me home to the Eternal Mother
    today

At your service anyway,
    (and until)

From MEXICO CITY BLUES
30TH CHORUS

Tender is the Night
Tender is the Eve Star

F. Scott Fitzgerald, the Alamoan
    Huckster Crockett Hero
    Who burned his Wife Down
    and tore up the 95 Devils
    with crashes of laughter
    and breaking of glass
    in the monocled Ibyarritz
    the Little Grey Fox
    OF NEW HAVEN CONN
    via Princeton   O Sure

Tender is the marlin spike,
    Tender is the sea,
  Tender the London Fog
    That Befalls to Me

Tender is the Cat's Bath
Blue Meow
The Little Grey Fox
    That nibbled at the grapes
Tender was his foreskin,
    tender his Nape.

36TH CHORUS

No direction
No direction to go

Burroughs says it's a time-space
    travel ship
Connected with mystiques
    and mysteries
Of he claims transcendental
    majesties,
Pulque green crabapples
    of hypnotic dream
In hanging Ecuad vine.
Burroughs says, We have destiny,
Last of the Faustian Men.

            No direction in the void
            Is the news from the void
            In touch with the void
            Everywhere void

No direction to go
            (but)
                    (in) ward

Hm
    (ripping of paper indicates
    helplessness anyway)

74TH CHORUS

"Darling!"
Red hot.
That kind of camping
I dont object to
unless it's kept
within reason.

"The coffee is delicious."

This is for Vidal

Didnt know I was
a Come-Onner, did you?
   (Come-on-er)

I am one of the world's
Great Bullshitters,
Girls

Very High Cantos

104TH CHORUS

I'd rather be thin than famous,
I dont wanta be fat,
And a woman throws me outa bed
Callin me Gordo, & everytime
                    I bend
                    to pickup
                    my suspenders
                    from the davenport
                    floor I explode
                    loud huge grunt-o
                    and disgust
                    every one
                    in the familio

    I'd rather be thin than famous
    But I'm fat

Paste that in yr. Broadway Show

190TH CHORUS

What I have attained in Buddhism
    is nothing.
What I wish to attain,
    is nothing.

Let me explain.
In perceiving the Dharma
    I achieved nothing—
What worries me is not
    nothing
But everything, the trouble is
    number,
But since everything is nothing
    then I am worried nil.
In seeking to attain the Dharma
    I failed, attaining nothing,
And so I succeeded the goal,
Which was, pure happy
    nothing.
No matter how you cut it
    it's empty delightful boloney

213TH CHORUS

Poem dedicated to Allen Ginsberg
—prap—rot—rort—
mort—port—lort—snort
—pell mell—rhine wine—
roll royce—ring ming—
mock my lot—roll my doll—
pull my hairline—smell my kell—
wail my siren—pile my ane—
loose my shoetongue—sing my aim—
loll my wildmoll—roll my
                        luck—
lay my cashier gone amuk—
suck my lamppole, raise the bane,
            hang the traitor
            inside my brain
        Fill my pail well,
ding my bell, smile for the ladies,
                come from hell

239TH CHORUS

Charley Parker Looked like Buddha
Charley Parker, who recently died
Laughing at a juggler on the TV
after weeks of strain and sickness,
was called the Perfect Musician.
And his expression on his face
Was as calm, beautiful, and profound
As the image of the Buddha
Represented in the East, the lidded eyes,
The expression that says "All is Well"
—This was what Charley Parker
Said when he played, All is Well.
You had the feeling of early-in-the-morning
Like a hermit's joy, or like
                    the perfect cry
Of some wild gang at a jam session
"Wail, Wop"—Charley burst
His lungs to reach the speed
Of what the speedsters wanted
And what they wanted
Was his Eternal Slowdown.
A great musician and a great
                    creator of forms
That ultimately find expression
In mores and what have you.

"I DREAMED OF A BUM SEVEN FOOT TALL"

I dreamed of a bum seven foot tall
That crushed the bourgeoisie to the cross.
He kissed me in the maple shot square
And then walked on.

Spartacus my tortured brother
If I should find you bussing crockery out of Bickford's
Or sunk beneath the 6th Ave El
Where it curves West 3rd Street into the twenties
The pillared zebra bold upon your whited chest . . .

Give me a signal by your delusions
Hallucinate Rome! The centurions in trouble
They cast a flame in your antique face
And wrestle your eyes for tomorrow's longing

While bread and roses rot in the streets
And lovers prepare their ecstatic excuses
I shall walk to the Battery
Now not tomorrow
The waves of the present
Smash from the sea.

Let the boat of your longing into great chaos
Ark out of vision
Love in the wind

"MY MUSE GOOSED ME"
For Sylvia (Pen-Pal)

My muse goosed me
In the middle of the night
(I had a terrible fright)
For as I fumbled for my pen (as was my wont)
I touched my wife upon her cont.
And dropped my muse upon the floor
Where she clattered around with an awful roar
As you can see by the words and meters of this poem
Then my wife came & took me home.

"IT IS LONELY"

      It is lonely

I must draw water from the well   75 buckets for the
    bath
I mix a drink—gin, fizz water, lemon juice, a spoonful
    of strawberry jam

And place it in a champagne glass—it is hard work
      to make the bath

And my winter clothes are dusty and should be
    put away

In storage.   Have I lost all values I wonder
      the world is slippery to hold on to

When you begin to deny it.

Outside outside are the crickets and frogs in the
    rice fields

Large black butterflies like birds.

JOANNE KYGER   129

"MY FATHER DIED THIS SPRING"

My father died this spring
    Well, I had meant to write more often
To a kind of hell it must be, with all unresolved
    difficulties.
  I had greens with vinegar last night—that's
something in common
    And I would have told him that—adding it to a
  list of possible conversations
With the pictures on his dressing table of all his
  daughters
but he wasn't flinging out his arms to keep a soul there.
        You can't say he wasn't strange
  and difficult.
        How far does one go
to help a parent like a child—when he waits
  at the employees entrance in old clothes
      and I don't want him.
      Well he'll be there waiting
for me. Demands just, wanted, or not
    are to be met.
And let me see, yes the demon large
    impossible and yields without vanishing
  no power, no satisfaction
      sitting on the back porch drinking beer
      following me to the sick squirrels in the cellar.

And the material things, calling cards
    engraved watches, trunks that married life brings
        full of stuff
he left behind 10 years ago. The golf clubs. The fact is
    there was a man, a married man,
    and an old man. it's impossible to know.
        but blood does bring curiosity.

MAY 29

Something sent me back and forth across the room,
I didn't find what I looked for, I didn't know what it
was, why did I have to move.

The clarity of the image. I can't cease talking at the
dinner table. The two things are not related, but I do
not know what to say. In the visual world

I can see them trudging up the hill, I have never been
concerned with the pressure of sounds.

There was a long time in silence. For myself, I can tell
you that certain things give me limited pleasure for
short stretches of time.

But I do not know where to put them, they are sure to
die, later than I, being metal or wood, broken hinges
and chipped, the horses step on them, how far can they
be thrown and pounded.

"Beauty is so rare a thing." He is weak as I hold his arm
he leans on me as we walk by the ocean. We forgive you
for never giving him the gift he wanted. He died in the
park, out over the ocean he talked of music, it is him
I like the best.

I shall not do that again.

"IT'S A GREAT DAY"

It's a great day. Last night I visited my old
childhood town of Lake Bluff, Illinois. The
Creeley's and Philip Whalen were there. I took
a walk to Lake Michigan with Philip to see it all
built up in the form of a great amusement center.
Lost in its intricacies I go to work. Stepping out
a door I land in a great field and run a tractor up
and down the rows, not exactly enough, to be sure
and run back into the amusement center, donning my
waitress uniform on the way, before I get caught,
before I get caught. Oh Ladies of the Middle West,
how do your hands get rough. What is this self
I think I will lose if I leave what I know. Back
to the dark bedroom, and aimless unhappy adolescent
lives. Lacking any commitment to the actual living
ground, life becomes pointless in its urge for culture,
quote unquote, Art. There, I've said it, in all it's
simpleness—the best teacher lives outside, the best
teacher lives inside you, beating blood, breathing
air, the best teacher is alive.

From HYPODERMIC LIGHT

It's absurd I can't bring my soul to the eye of
    odoriferous fire

my soul whose teeth never leave their cadavers
my soul twisted on rocks of mental freeways
my soul that hates music
I would rather not see the Rose in my thoughts take on
    illusionary prerogatives
it is enough to have eaten bourgeois testicles
it is enough that the masses are all sodomites
Good Morning
the ships are in I've brought the gold to burn
    Moctezuma
I'm in a tipi joking with seers I'm smoking yahnah
I'm in a joint smoking marijuana with a cat who looks
    like Jesus Christ
heroin is a door always opened by white women
my first act of treason was to be born!
I'm at war with the Zodiac
my suffering comes on as a fire going out O beautiful
    world contemplation!

It's a fact my soul is smoking!

*

That the total hatred wants to annihilate me!
it's the sickness of american pus against which I'm
      hallucinated
I'm sick of language
I want this wall I see under my eyes break up and
      shatter you
I'm talking all the poems after God
I want the table of visions to send me oriole opium
A state of siege
It's possible to live directly from elementals! hell
      stamps out vegetable spirits, zombies attack
      heaven! the marvelous put down by martial law,
      America fucked by a stick of marijuana
paper money larded for frying corpses!

HERE comes the Gorgon! THERE'S the outhouse!

      Come up from dead things, anus of the sun!

HIGH

O beato solitudo! where have I flown to?
stars overturn the wall of my music
as flight of birds, they go by, the spirits
opened below the lark of plenty
ovens of neant overflow the docks at Veracruz
This much is time
summer coils the soft suck of night
lone unseen eagles crash thru mud
I am worn like an old sack by the celestial bum
I'm dropping my eyes where all the trees turn on fire!
I'm mad to go to you, Solitude—who will carry
        me there?
I'm wedged in this collision of planets/Tough!
I'm ONGED!
I'm the trumpet of King David
the sinister elevator tore itself limb by limb

                You can not close
                you can not open
                you break yr head
                you make bloody bread!

"MAN IS IN PAIN"

Man is in pain
    ten bright balls bat the air
    falling through the window
    on which his double leans a net the air made
    to catch the ten bright balls

Man is a room
    where the malefic hand turns a knob
    on the unseen unknown double's door

Man is in pain
    with his navel hook caught on a stone quarry
    where ten bright balls chose to land
    AND where the malefic hand carves
      on gelatinous air THE WINDOW
    to slam shut on his shadow's tail

    Ten bright balls bounce into the unseen
    unknown double's net
Man is a false window
    through which his double walks to the truth
    that falls as ten bright balls
    the malefic hand tossed into the air

Man is in pain
    ten bright spikes nailed to the door!

PHILIP LAMANTIA   137

THE GYPSY'S WINDOW

It seems a stage
backed by imaginations of velvet,
cotton, satin, loops and stripes—

A lovely unconcern
scattered the trivial plates, the rosaries
and centered
a narrownecked dark vase,
unopened yellow and pink
paper roses, a luxury of open red
paper roses—

Watching the trucks go by, from stiff chairs
behind the window show, an old
bandanna'd brutal dignified
woman, a young beautiful woman
her mouth a huge contemptuous rose—

The courage
of natural rhetoric tosses to dusty
Hudson St. the chance of poetry, a chance
poetry gives passion to the roses,
the roses in the gypsy's window in a blue
vase, look real, as unreal
as real roses.

THE FLIGHT*

    "The will is given us that
        we may know the
delights of surrender." Blake with
tense mouth, crouched small (great forehead,
somber eye) amid a crowd's tallness in a narrow room.
                The same night
a bird caught in my room, battered
from wall to wall, missing the window over & over
                    (till it gave up and
              huddled half-dead on a shelf, and I
              put up the sash against the cold)

and waking at dawn I again
pushed the window violently down, open
            and the bird gathered itself and flew
            straight out
            quick and calm (over the radiant
              chimneys—

*The quoted words were spoken by Blake in my dream.
This was London, 1945.—D.L.

THE MARRIAGE

You have my
attention: which is
a tenderness, beyond
what I may say. And I have
your constancy to
             something beyond myself.
The force
of your commitment charges us—we live
in the sweep of it, taking courage
one from the other.

THE MARRIAGE (II)

I want to speak to you.
To whom else should I speak?
It is you who make
a world to speak of.
In your warmth the
fruits ripen—all the
apples and pears that grow
on the south wall of my
head. If you listen
it rains for them, then
they drink. If you
speak in response
the seeds
jump into the ground.
Speak or be silent: your silence
will speak to me.

POEM FROM MANHATTAN

Green-spined
river-bounded
desired of summer storms

                    (city, act of joy

Spring evenings in sea-light
facades relax
steel & stone float among clouds

                    (city, act of power

And always nightfall flicks
fantasy on black air
       chips of light
flashing   scattered

                    (city, act of energy

Over littered avenues
& yawn of brakes at the lights
       hesitation of dawn
        dazed behind smoke feathers

                    (city, act of hope

But down, past many windows
        each holding less,
less light—
                down—
each weak pane tossing, feebly handing, letting drop
        pale suns to lower panes—
                        fall
        many fathoms down

                        (city, desolation

                fall
to cracks between cages
where men are walking
jostled, in dirty light
(reflected light)
are running

                        (city, gesture of greed

the derelict & the diamond-sharp
in shadow of inordinate monuments

It is to them
who speaks must speak

Precise
as rain's first
spitting words on the pavement
          pick out
                    the core
          lost impulse

                    (give it back

A VACANCY

An old unconsummated
Love . . . hangs sadly
In my thoughts.

When passion is gone,
The moment—unspent—
Stands silent, accusing,

An abortion, neither buried
Nor born—its space
A vacancy.

THE FLOWERS OF POLITICS (I)

THIS IS THE HUGE DREAM OF US THAT WE
ARE HEROS THAT THERE IS COURAGE
in our blood! That we are live!
That we do not perpetrate the lie of vision
forced upon ourselves
by ourselves. That we have made the nets of vision real!
AND SNARED THEM

OH I AM BLIND AS A FLOWER AND SENSE LESS
we see nothing but banality.
Break in the forms and take real postures!

This is the real world clear and open.
The flower moves and motion is its sense,
and transference of ions
all that it does is perception
and vision.
OH BREAK UP THE FORMS AND FEEL NEW
THINGS
I declare that I am love who have never known
it and I make new love.
My hand is pink and white and blue and great
to me. My eyes are bright
and I know that love is air. An act
and nothing more. That we are seraphs,

cherubim and heros, chieftains and gods.
This is the blind senseless thing of knowing
that unconscious we walk in it, and strive
among all things. This is
A CANDLE
and shape of light.
The hand and arm annunciate all things

and draw the eye upon the speaking face

declaring from the inner body.
We are wrought on a bending shaft of air and light
and make an animal around it

and spread a radiance from ourselves that melts
in light.

THE FLOWERS OF POLITICS (II)

ONLY WHAT IS HEROIC AND COURAGEIOUS
MOVES OUR BLOOD
we are lost within ourselves and tangles
of a narrow room and world if we do not speak out,
reach out
and strive from individuality. This is

WHAT I HEAR IN HEART NERVES LUNGS,
NOT ELEGIES.
I am a black beast and clear man in one. With no
split or division. But from one without.
AND WALK IN IT FREE
as flowers or blood
and hate the forms of it you make
destroying it to take it from my touch
and sight. I hate
you in the night when I am whole and free.
And I know you will be stamped out by your forms
and invisible revolutions and I

do what I will and can to speed them on.
THOSE LEFT WILL BE GODS AND SERAPHIM
and need no memory of you—
only this is more than beauty
without holiness and self-conceit.

Your sickness poisons you and you
are dying. No aid
or speed can save you. And I
am free!

Free of politics. Liberty and pride to guide you.
You pass
from ancestral myths to myth of self. And make
the giant bright stroke like that madman Van Gogh.

MAD SONNET 13
For Allen Ginsberg

ON COLD SATURDAY I WALKED IN THE
EMPTY VALLEY OF WALL STREET.
I dreamed with the hanging concrete eagles
and I spoke with the black-bronze foot of Washington.
I strode in the vibrations
of money-strength
in the narrow, cold, lovely CHASM.

Oh perfect chill slot of space!

WALL STREET, WALL STREET,
MOUNTED WITH DEAD BEASTS AND MEN
and metal placards greened and darkened.
AND A CATHEDRAL AT YOUR HEAD!

I see that the men are alive and born
and inspired
by the moving beauty of their (own) physical figures
who will tear
the vibrations-of-strength from the vibrations-
of-money
and drop them like a dollar on the chests
of the Senate!
They step with the pride of a continent.

FROM THE UNTITLED EPIC POEM

Somewhere, waiting to be found; a bar-mitzvah of hope-lessness in the Waldorf Cafeteria, hungering for a chance to detonate New York, return the Masses to themselves; hungering, waiting to be found, rejoicing in Joyce because he confused, little magazines because they refused, rejecting the scholar who seemed too safe, all-knowing; sitting in the Waldorf Cafeteria wonder-ing where Bohemia was, in some back alley of the Village waiting to be stumbled into.

Youngest radical to join the back lines, waiting for a chance to step out of line and proclaim an action that never happened; to throw a bomb into the marble echo of a Bank, or tie TNT to the Brooklyn Bridge at rush hour, to topple the statue of George Washington in Wall Street; start a chain-reaction of burning dresses in the Garment Center; to free the enslaved; enslave the enslavers; to do anything, but to do some-thing final.

Folk-singing prophets in mid-afternoon: sandal squeaking ventriloquists of the proletariat; Zionist zom-bies sipping espresso; Itkin, the impossible, on the steps of a Catholic Church, confused by Eliot, wishing he wasn't queer; the lisp and laugh of fairies snipping perfume through the streets; sequin bitchery, the tough humor of survivors; night of blackened days, Benzedrine blues, and early morning flowers on the street, walking home and stepping on scattered petals.

Black uniforms; danced in the Waldorf, turned-on in the Automat, threw ourselves in front of the A train; we were living visions of weekly suicides, crawling into hangouts with dripping bandages.

Somewhere, waiting to be found, we fooled the fakirs, were kings of the underworld; maggots in some armpit; no loving, only the desire for love, and the waiting.

Genesis one, the beginning; we would go away, discover Zen, Spiritualism, the positive, the negative, whisper of Sartre and the Paris Existentialism. I followed, failed to find, and no one celebrated my bar-mitzvah in the Waldorf Cafeteria, not even myself.

6TH RAGA: FOR BOB ALEXANDER

Cigarette gone, you walked over
to the stain where the sea last hit
the shore and, with your fingers,
drew the outline of a woman.
Her breasts, a poke inside each center
for her nipples; her cunt,
a simple v, and her hair
a spray of seaweed found nearby.

Jumping back, the sea rushing in,
you yelled something I didn't hear.
We turned our backs to the Pacific,
back up to Ocean Front Avenue.
Charlie was waiting with his camera.
Altoon arrived with a six-pack of
good old Lucky Lager beer.

DAVID MELTZER   153

15TH RAGA: FOR BELA LUGOSI

Sir, when you say
Transylvania or wolfbane or
I am Count Dracula,
your eyes widen &, for the moment,
become pure white marble.

No wonder you were a junkie.
It's in the smile. Your way of drifting
into Victorian bedrooms
holding up your cape like skirts,
then covering her face
as you bent over to kiss & sup.

It is no wonder & it was
in good taste too.

PICASSO VISITS BRAQUE

Picasso flies into a rage at Braque,
screaming, You have stolen my jaws!
bastard, give back my browns!
my noses! my guitars!

Braque, puffing his pipe,
continues painting in silence.
Aha! yells Picasso. Roast duck!
I smell roast duck!
Aren't you even inviting me for lunch?

Wordlessly, Braque puffs and paints.

You know, says Picasso, more amiably,
that's a pretty good job you're doing there, Georges.
Tell me, isn't that duck finished yet?

Voracious, Picasso is ready to devour the duck, the
        canvas, the other guests.
But Braque only squints at his painting,
adding a dash of color here and there.

Disgruntled, Picasso slaps his mistress, boils his
        secretary in oils, casts a withering look at the art
        dealer trembling in a corner and

laughs,
biting the air
with 4 huge rows of teeth
blinking malevolently
3 eyes

I WOULD NOT RECOMMEND LOVE

                              my head felt stabbed
by a crown of thorns but I joked and rode the subway
and ducked into school johns to masturbate
and secretly wrote
                    of teenage hell
because I was "different"
the first and last of my kind
smothering acute sensations
in swimming pools and locker rooms
addict of lips and genitals
mad for buttocks
                    that Whitman and Lorca
and Catullus and Marlowe
                              and Michelangelo
and Socrates admired

and I wrote: Friends,
if you wish to survive
I would not recommend
Love

"I HAVE ALWAYS LIKED GEORGE GERSHWIN MORE THAN ERNEST HEMINGWAY"

I have always liked George Gershwin more than Ernest
    Hemingway
    tho they both meant Paris when I grew like a tree in
      Brooklyn
        & the sun also rose
                  on my disgruntlement
with a loud clunk that could be heard from Prospect Park to
    Gravesend Bay
    a considerable distance
                 little did I imagine then
           that I'd cross the Great Water and sit
           sipping pernod with Gershwin's
                sister-in-law and *Porgy*
                    excitement of brainwaves

I HAVE SEEN THE LIGHT
AND IT IS MY MIND

the State has decided: who I am to love, to hate
what I'm to do in bed, with what and to whom

the State has made a military coup in bed
stop screaming: the world is a better place

we are now going to sing the virtues of mass murder
we will follow our religious leaders

our feelings are stamped: State Property
pornography is practiced by God
who has raped more souls than you can shake a prick at

Jesus Christ is a funny name
for an hallucinogenic drug

all those addicts like Billy Graham and the Pope
will have to account for their expensive habit

from his last words on the cross
I gather Jesus was begging for the ultimate fix

HAROLD NORSE   159

HOTEL NIRVANA

1

if only by pronouncing SHIVA
   if by repetition of the mantra
      by endlessly chanting a delightful phrase my liver
         spleen
                   heart intestines
         could suddenly be restored whole

if all the vicious circles of resistance & violence could be
dissolved by the powerful sound of a universal OM
     uttered
from the beginning of the kosmos to the end of the kalpas

ah my god   watching the white smoke of the locomotive
     in the
valley at night the gloomy cliffs the lights of the village
ghostly veils of milky silvering blackness gone in a puff

watching my fright & panic on waking in darkness with
     a terrible
dream of loneness like death coming on

watching the soothing effect of a mantra repeated till the
sound reverberates thru all my cells turning them to
     jewels
of momentary glinting light

watching myself in all my manifest mazes

watching a tidal wave of giant stars & flowers & flames
   & wheels whirling disks in the sky
space beyond space   endlessly
    opening my human head
past all limits with body still on earth among houses
    & trees
        & the sun the sun
        with calm full gaze
                & the moon her lunar eyes
                  stillness raying
                      astral influences

watching medieval woodcuts viols flutes hautboys
    flageolets lutes
pure voices of faith & holy peace & plaques
   mottled faces the barrows loaded with corpses
   nuns with habits over their bellies flung on the ground
      getting fucked by monks
        they all have eternal expressions
          emotionless faint smiles
              of passion as if posed in monalisa
              noncommittal
                disinterested mystery

o benevolent passion that lifts us on magic carpets out the
windows of middleclass tenements! that raises us on
    waves
of our own minds
                        out of our mind limits
o molecular rainbow!
o carafe where tiny sperms swim!
o lies of love & brotherhood!
o emotional bullshit!
                    leaving only the cold fact
                the desert
                the child crying again
                    man betrayed again

      if only by pronouncing a syllable
        if by casting a spell
        I could hold off
          the bold girl who stole
            flesh from my flesh

who tore my spirit up
and left me with knocking knees
heaving guts
and gagging throat
threatened with void

      my break with a thousand loves in one

2

i am gnawing the bark of trees in hunger
 i am getting furious at everybody
  i am the screaming kingdom of torn up streets of
   earthquake
   i am hate which i call love
    i am the poet of potential murder
i am the post office of athens losing important letters
 i am tying up millions of lives in knots & vicious circles
  i am kafka midas labyrinth of lost souls with no
   thread back
i am death destruction annihilation emptiness ignorance
  dreams evil
 i am smoking & drinking myself to death
  i cannot learn my lesson
   i am a nasty prolonged illness
    i am a whitehaired old lady who thinks she
     is god
i am the terrible endless persecution of the individual
  by the state
i am red tape cancer cigarettes blackmail lying theft
  disgust
 i am white light breaking thru gloom
  i am gloom breaking thru white light
   i am my cat lapping her nounou
    i con myself with cynical ruthlessness

i steal cars & rape children & run an eternal racket to
        grab while the grabbing is good
    i am available in small doses only
        i breathe the poisons of noisy overcrowded cities
            i am contradiction separation loneliness
i am the soul yearning for god who does not exist
        except in myself

PERSONAL POEM

Now when I walk around at lunchtime
I have only two charms in my pocket
an old Roman coin Mike Kanemitsu gave me
and a bolt-head that broke off a packing case
when I was in Madrid the others never
brought me too much luck though they did
help keep me in New York against coercion
but now I'm happy for a time and interested

I walk through the luminous humidity
passing the House of Seagram with its wet
and its loungers and the construction to
the left that closed the sidewalk if
I ever get to be a construction worker
I'd like to have a silver hat please
and get to Moriarty's where I wait for
LeRoi and hear who wants to be a mover and
shaker the last five years my batting average
is .016 that's that, and LeRoi comes in
and tells me Miles Davis was clubbed 12
times last night outside BIRDLAND by a cop
a lady asks us for a nickel for a terrible
disease but we don't give her one we
don't like terrible diseases, then
we go eat some fish and some ale it's

cool but crowded we don't like Lionel Trilling
we decide, we like Don Allen we don't like
Henry James so much we like Herman Melville
we don't want to be in the poets' walk in
San Francisco even we just want to be rich
and walk on girders in our silver hats
I wonder if one person out of the 8,000,000 is
thinking of me as I shake hands with LeRoi
and buy a strap for my wristwatch and go
back to work happy at the thought possibly so

AUTOBIOGRAPHIA LITERARIA

When I was a child
I played by myself in a
corner of the schoolyard
all alone.

I hated dolls and I
hated games, animals were
not friendly and birds
flew away.

If anyone was looking
for me I hid behind a
tree and cried out "I am
an orphan."

And here I am, the
center of all beauty!
writing these poems!
Imagine!

FRANK O'HARA

TODAY

Oh! kangaroos, sequins, chocolate sodas!
You really are beautiful! Pearls,
harmonicas, jujubes, aspirins! all
the stuff they've always talked about
still makes a poem a surprise!
These things are with us every day
even on beachheads and biers. They
do have meaning. They're strong as rocks.

MY HEART

I'm not going to cry all the time
nor shall I laugh all the time,
I don't prefer one "strain" to another.
I'd have the immediacy of a bad movie,
not just a sleeper, but also the big,
overproduced first-run kind. I want to be
at least as alive as the vulgar. And if
some aficionado of my mess says "That's
not like Frank!", all to the good! I
don't wear brown and grey suits all the time,
do I? No. I wear workshirts to the opera,
often. I want my feet to be bare,
I want my face to be shaven, and my heart—
you can't plan on the heart, but
the better part of it, my poetry, is open.

AVENUE A

We hardly ever see the moon any more
                                        so no wonder
   it's so beautiful when we look up suddenly
and there it is gliding broken-faced over the bridges
brilliantly coursing, soft, and a cool wind fans
      your hair over your forehead and your memories
         of Red Grooms' locomotive landscape
I want some bourbon/you want some oranges/I love
      the leather jacket Norman gave me
                              and the corduroy coat David
   gave you, it is more mysterious than spring, the
      El Greco
heavens breaking open and then reassembling like lions
                                 in a vast tragic veldt
   that is far from our small selves and our temporally
         united
passions in the cathedral of Januaries

   everything is too comprehensible
these are my delicate and caressing poems
I suppose there will be more of those others to come,
      as in the past
                     so many!
but for now the moon is revealing itself like a pearl
                        to my equally naked heart

NOW THAT I AM IN MADRID
AND CAN THINK

I think of you
and the continents brilliant and arid
and the slender heart you are sharing my share of with
    the American air
as the lungs I have felt sonorously subside slowly greet
    each morning
and your brown lashes flutter revealing two perfect
    dawns colored by New York

see a vast bridge stretching to the humbled outskirts
    with only you
  standing on the edge of the purple like an only tree

and in Toledo the olive groves' soft blue look at the
    hills with silver
  like glasses like an old lady's hair
it's well known that God and I don't get along together
it's just a view of the brass works to me, I don't care
    about the Moors
seen through you the great works of death, you are
    greater

you are smiling, you are emptying the world so we can
    be alone

FRANK O'HARA   171

HAVING A COKE WITH YOU

is even more fun than going to San Sebastian, Irún,
      Hendaye, Biarritz, Bayonne
or being sick to my stomach on the Travesera de
      Gracia in Barcelona
partly because in your orange shirt you look like a
      better happier St. Sebastian
partly because of my love for you, partly because of
      your love for yoghurt
partly because of the fluorescent orange tulips around
      the birches
partly because of the secrecy our smiles take on before
      people and statuary
it is hard to believe when I'm with you that there can
      be anything as still
as solemn as unpleasantly definitive as statuary when
      right in front of it
in the warm New York 4 o'clock light we are drifting
      back and forth
between each other like a tree breathing through its
      spectacles

and the portrait show seems to have no faces in it at all,
      just paint

you suddenly wonder why in the world anyone ever
    did them
                I look
at you and I would rather look at you than all the
    portraits in the world
except possibly for the *Polish Rider* occasionally and
    anyway it's in the Frick
which thank heavens you haven't gone to yet so we can
    go together the first time
and the fact that you move so beautifully more or less
    takes care of Futurism
just as at home I never think of the *Nude Descending a
    Staircase* or
at a rehearsal a single drawing of Leonardo or
    Michelangelo that used to wow me
and what good does all the research of the
    Impressionists do them
when they never got the right person to stand near the
    tree when the sun sank
or for that matter Marino Marini when he didn't pick
    the rider as carefully as the horse
            it seems they were all cheated of some
                marvelous experience
which is not going to go wasted on me which is why
    I'm telling you about it

PETER'S JEALOUS OF ALLEN

Had a trauma-like dream last night
as I was sleeping on Ansen's roof—
I saw 4 comets jive fastly across the sky
before falling asleep thinking what the world
will be like when roket ships are invented, what
will happen to our world if we discover another
world of people we can treat as slaves? and on, and
on—then I fall asleep and dream
that I am in a big room with about 5 other people,
for some reason I feel extreemly uneasy, Allen
is in the room, he is cooking & so is walking
back & forth—there are some other poets in the room,
one elderly poet had a book in his hand, reading, I dont
know who they were but all regarded Allen as
the most important person in the room.
I am standing around doing nothing—there seems to be
a stream running thro the room, which is bare
except for couch, chairs, and a closset whare my
gray coat is. Allen is cooking & for some reason
I tackle him, he falls on the floor & I fall on
his legs—he had a plate of grapes in his hand
& they spilled all over the floor—He turns over &
looks at me—his whole face changed—gaunt, like
Bill Burroughs—with high cheekbones—he looked
angry—& said—"Why did you do that? here I am cooking,

is that all you can do?" His face was mad at me.
I was scared, frightened & ancious to prove my worth
to all these poets reading, but I couldent, I felt
they dident like me & thought me mad. I felt they
        dident
care about me—I was all ancious. I remember this part
of the dream best—My arms were swinging—I would
fold one hand into the other, rubbing them into one
        another.
My nerves were at the end. I wanted to get away from
this group of poets & so ran to the closit
for my slick gray coat—to of put that on would
of ment cutting off relations with Allen, so I dident.
I put the coat back, & tried to sit down but couldent
& so I walked about the room like Roskolnikoff, feeling
all alone & mad in the world—that was it.
When I woke up in the morning thinking about
the dream, I had a fantasy—that ran—
I could of done something else in that dream—
& I fantisized taking a knife & making
a big cut in my bicept musle
in the upper arm—then they all got up
to get the knife from me—but
I wanted to bleed to death slowly in front of them—
for here I would be the main figure of attention

& not Allen—or the other poets—& as they came
closser—I waved the knife at them
& said—"cant you leave a dying man in peece—
get away—" & they wouldent—so
I plunged the big blade into my neck bone
& down into my heart—& died
slowly—telling them all
what I felt about them.

"WRITING POEMS IS A SAINTLY THING"

Writing poems is a Saintly thing, the heart bursts like
    feeding red chickens on a green hill, or sitting on a
    balloon comming down to a window sill in time for
      morning to welcome me
          into your early rise of bacon & rolls & that tune
              on the
radio for dancing around the kitchen tabol
                     with spoons in yr mouth.
One room is all I'll ever own in eternity, one bed—
                   Memory   ramblings
over tall mountains carrying me away to that nomads
    land whare to breathe is but to sigh at a lost
    dream that
                 rolls away from the eyes—
Rain & snow a clock on my window What good is my
    room it cant hold
    all the people in the world and chairs lonely because
    built for only one?
I tell you youth wants more of this world than our
    farthers left us.
          A mirror makes two & that's a blessing.
Grinding my teeth for lack of love, walking into a
    cathedral is like walking into a cold stove, like into
    a glove.

I know the angel behind the door will bring me good
     paintings before long.
All angels meet on the curve of the earth & form a line
     that becomes a bridge to the sun.

SOME ONE LIKED ME WHEN
I WAS TWELVE

When I was a kid in summer camp,
around 13teen & one night I lay asleep
in bunglow bed with 13teen other boys,
when in comes one of the camp councilors
who is nice fellow that likes ya, comeing to
my bed, sits down & starts to say: now you
will be leaving soon back to Flushing & I may never
        see you
again—but if theres ever aneything I

can do to help ya let me know, my farther is
a lawyer & I live at such & such a place
& this is my adress—I like you very much—
& if yr ever alone in the world come to me.
So I loked at him getting sad & tuched &
then years latter like now, 28, laying on
bed, my hunney-due mellon Allen sleeping next to me
—I realize he was quear & wanted my
flesh meat & my sweetness of that age—
that we just might of given each other.

COLLABORATION: LETTER TO
CHARLIE CHAPLIN

Our Dear Friend Charles:

Love letter for you. We are one happy poet & one
unhappey poet in India which makes 2 poets. We would
like come visit you when we get thru India to tickle yr
feet. Further more King in New York is great picture,—
I figure it will take about 10 yrs before it looks funny
in perspective. Every few years we dream in our sleep
we meat you.

Why dont you go ahead & make another picture & fuck
everybody. If you do could we be Extras. We be yr
Brownies free of charge.

Let us tell you about Ganesha. He is elephant-faced god
with funney fat belley human body. Everyone in India
has picture of him in their house. To think of him brings
happey wisdom success that he gives after he eats his
sweet candey. He neither exists nor does not exist.
Because of that he can conquer aney demon. He rides
around on a mouse & has 4 hands. We salute yr comedy
in his name.

Do you realize how maney times we have seen yr
pictures in Newark & cried in the dark at the roses. Do
you realize how maney summers in Coney Island we
sat in open air theatre & watched you disguised as a

lamp-shade in scratchey down stairs eternity. You even made our dead mothers laugh. So, remember everything is alright. We await your next move & the world still depends on yr *next move*.

What else shall we say to you before we all die? If everything we feel could be said it would be very beautiful. Why didnt we ever do this before? I guess the world seems so vast, its hard to find the right moment to forget all about this shit & wave hello from the other side of the earth. But there is certainly millions & millions of people waveing hello to you silently all over the windows, streets & movies. Its only life waveing to its self.

Tell Michael to read our poems too if you ever get them. Again we say you got that personal tickle-tuch we like-love.

Shall we let it go at that?

NO, we still got lots more room on the page—we still to emptey our hearts. Have you read Louis Ferdinand Celine?—hes translated into english from French— Celine vomits Rasberries. He wrote the most Chaplinesque prose in Europe & he has a bitter mean sad uggly eternal comical soul enough to make you cry.

You could make a great picture about the Atom Bomb!

Synops:

a grubby old janitor with white hair who cant get the air-raid drill instructions right & goes about his own lost business in the basement in the midst of great international air-raid emergencies, sirens, kremlin riots, flying rockets, radios screaming, destruction of the earth. He comes out the next day, he cralls out of the pile of human empire state building bodies, & the rest of the picture, a hole hour the janitor on the screen alone makeing believe he is being sociable with nobody there, haveing a beer at the bar with invisible boys, reading last years newspapers, & ending looking blankly into the camera with the eternal aged Chaplin-face looking blankly, raptly into the eyes of the God of Solitude.

There is yr fitting final statement Sir Chaplin, you will save the world if ya make it—but yr final look must be so beautiful that it doesnt matter if the world is saved or not.

Okay I guess we can end it now. Forgive us if you knew it all before. Okay

> Love & Flowers
> Peter Orlovsky, Allen Ginsberg
> *1961 Bombay*

TAKE MY DISPROPORTIONATE DESIRE

Enough of expressionist flowers lions and wheat,
Let us consider our separate needs
Here in this beautiful city of delicate surfaces
That a touch makes bleed.

Bring me that truth love-ridden whose black
     blaze makes
A comfort in the ice-bitten ghettos of cities, that wise
Love whose intemperate told truth thrusts into
     the aching
Arms of old men old women's lonely bodies with a cry.

All lovers, even lucky, need such intransigence as stays
Wrecked harborers who together cough, drink, spit
Gay blood into the gutter. I need that passion, miracle,
Incautious faith. To only you I offer it.

MATINS & LAUDS

Excited as a sophisticated boy at his first
Passion of intellect, aware and fully free
Having lost title to full liberty; struck
Aware, for once, as I would always be;

It day and I still shaken, still sure, see
It is not ring-magic nor the faithing leap of sex
That makes me your woman; marks our free
And separate wills with one intent; sets
My each earlier option at dazzling apex
And at naught; cancels, paid, all debts.
Restless, incautious, I want to talk violence,
Speak wild poems, hush, be still, pray grace
Taken forever; and after, lie long in the dense
Dark of your embrace, asleep between earth and space.

COMMUNION OF SAINTS: THE POOR BASTARD UNDER THE BRIDGE

The arrows of the narrow moon flock down direct
Into that looking heart by Seine walls unprotected.
Moonward the eyes of that hurt head still will
Stare and scarcely see the moonlight spill
Because black Notre Dame between her towers
Strikes home to him the third of this day's hours
And he, now man, heaped a cold afaint
Below the Pont Marie will, with a shout,
Enlist among the triumphant when Poor Saint
Julien's bells will clock out
Four.

      In his rags, unchapleted, almost astray
Among the dead packed all immaculate away
Under the city, he awaits his sentry
The four o'clock moon to warrant for his entry
                     o and pure
The pure in children's ranks by bells immured
In gowns of light will singing telling rise
Unfold their arms impelled without surprise
Will lift up flowered laurel, will walk out
Among their golden singing like a victor's shout
To their triumphant heaven's golden ringing brim
And welcome welcome welcome him.

EASTER SATURDAY, NY, NY

Confusion of bells, and all the starling sky
Is shouting, even the gloved policemen are laughing
Because you turn again.

You chose despair, were darkened, now changed you
Chosen veer; you choose; you are; God knows
There's no despair could quiet you. There is
This afterward, this new now abolishing
Your proven death   o darling
How the city rings with light, sheer
Stone is diamond, all perfect squares
Flare into tropics of flowers, the rush of the roller
Skating children tunnels into singing. Our
Loss, impeached, dies off clever and devious;
It was too magic, too untrue. Triumph
Up the avenue sounds trumpets and roses;
The tallest buildings blaze all night and dancing
Is everywhere under the sidestreet trees.

ROCKEFELLER THE CENTER

Roland is dead and the ivory broken
Marie has forgotten the limb-striking end of joy.

    Pigeons patter, whirr, at the copy cathedral;
       a Prometheus
    Aeschylus did not intend submits to sparrows,
               less than ever free;
    At his manufactured feet the delicate ice-skaters
      swirl.

    A paralleled curve incised among angles, the
      splendid loose
    Avenue ripples with peopled cars, and the
      figuring girl
    Looks at the sky beyond the sidewalk's ginko tree.

Though the sea-coves echo with innumerable
Voices no man suspects the vanished Neirids.

Artemis at midnight is
No longer solicited.

MIGRATION OF BIRDS

It started just now with a hummingbird
Hovering over the porch two yards away
                              then gone,
It stopped me studying.
I saw the redwood post
Leaning in clod ground
Tangled in a bush of yellow flowers
Higher than my head, through which we push
Every time we come inside—
The shadow network of the sunshine
Through its vines. White-crowned sparrows
Make tremendous singings in the trees
The rooster down the valley crows and crows.
Jack Kerouac outside, behind my back
Reads the *Diamond Sutra* in the sun.
Yesterday I read *Migration of Birds*;
The Golden Plover and the Arctic Tern.
Today that big abstraction's at our door
For juncoes and the robins all have left,
Broody scrabblers pick up bits of string
And in this hazy day
Of April summer heat
Across the hill the seabirds
Chase Spring north along the coast:
Nesting in Alaska
In six weeks.

A SINECURE FOR P. WHALEN

Whalen, curious vulture,
Picked the Western mind,
Ate the cataracted eyes
That once saw Gwion race the hag
And addle gentlemen

Still unfilled, he skittered to
The sweet bamboo
Fed green on yellow silt
And built a poem to dead Li Po.
The Drunkard taught him how to dance,
Leave dead bodies to the plants,
Sleep out nights in rain.

UNDER THE SKIN OF IT

Naturally tender, flesh and such
Being entirely mortal, fragile
And complex as a model plane.
Demanding attention, in its unfair ways

Getting, of course, the pleasure that it seeks.

But is it pleased?
Flesh being a type of clay (or dust);
Spirit, the other, like a gas,
Rising and floating in the hollow
Of the Skull—

Which is to know the other's real delight?

Both under the skin, which stretches
As we grow, sagging a trifle
In the pinch of time. Enchanting
The thought of pleasure pleasing flesh and bone.

AUGUST ON SOURDOUGH, A VISIT
FROM DICK BREWER

You hitched a thousand miles
                    north from San Francisco
Hiked up the mountainside   a mile in the air
The little cabin—one room—
                    walled in glass
Meadows and snowfields,   hundreds of peaks.
We lay in our sleeping bags
                    talking half the night;
Wind in the guy-cables   summer mountain rain.
Next morning I went with you
                    as far as the cliffs,
Loaned you my poncho—   the rain across the shale—
You down the snowfield
                    flapping in the wind
Waving a last goodbye   half hidden in the clouds
To go on hitching
                    clear to New York;
Me back to my mountain   and far, far, west.

HOW THE SESTINA (YAWN) WORKS

I opened this poem with a yawn
thinking how tired I am of revolution
the way it's presented on television
isn't exactly poetry
You could use some more methedrine
if you ask me personally

People should be treated personally
there's another yawn
here's some more methedrine
Thanks! Now about this revolution
What do you think? What is poetry?
Is it like television?

Now I get up and turn off the television
Whew! It was getting to me personally
I think it is like poetry
Yawn   it's 4 A.M. yawn   yawn
This new record is one big revolution
if you were listening you'd understand methedrine

isn't the greatest drug no not methedrine
it's no fun for watching television
You want to jump up have a revolution
about something that affects you personally

192

When you're busy and involved you never yawn
it's more like feeling, like energy, like poetry

I really like to write poetry
it's more fun than grass, acid, THC, methedrine
If I can't write I start to yawn
and it's time to sit back, watch television
see what's happening to me personally:
war, strike, starvation, revolution

This is a sample of my own revolution
taking the easy way out of poetry
I want it to hit you all personally
like a shot of extra-strong methedrine
so you'll become your own television
Become your own yawn!

O giant yawn, violent revolution
silent television, beautiful poetry
most deadly methedrine
                    I choose all of you for my poem personally

ANNE WALDMAN   193

REVOLUTION

Spooky summer on the horizon I'm gazing at
from my window into the streets
That's where it's going to be where everyone is
walking around, looking around out in the open
suspecting each other's heart to open fire
all over the streets
                     like streets you read about every day
who are the network we travel through on the way to
     the center
which is energy filling life
and bursting with joy all over the screen
                           I can't sit still any longer!

I want to go where I'm not feeling so bad
Get off this little island before the bridges break
(my heart is a sore thing too)
No I want to sit in the middle watching movies
then go to bed in my head
Someone is banging on it with a heavy stick like the enemy
who is he going to be turns into a face you can't recognize
then vanishes behind a window behind a gun
Like the lonely hero stalking the main street
cries out Where are you? I just want to know
all the angles of death possible under the American sky!

I can hardly see for all the buildings polluting the sky
until it changes into a barrage of bottles
then clears up for a second while you breathe
and you realize you're still as alive as ever and want to be
but would like to be somewhere else perhaps Africa
Start all over again as the race gets darker and darker
and the world goes on the way I always thought it would
For the winner is someone we recognize out of our
        collective past
which is turning over again in the grave

        It is so important when one dies you replace her
        and never waste a minute

DIARIES

Martha was a girl after my own heart. She slept late, lived for the moment, and did the thing. Now this was the truth. We had not known each other long before we discovered the common bonds. One day was like this in the diary:

> Got up late. Here I am writing in the diary. It is 1:00 P.M. It is raining outside. Martha is coming over (soon I hope). The coffee is boiling so I have to go.

Later she showed me her diary:

> Raining outside. Just got up. 1:00 P.M. Going over to X's soon. Coffee is ready.

Then I showed her my diary even later and we agreed that we had much in common. I asked her about the X, however, and she said, "You can never tell can you who might see it?"

I agreed and since then have been using arbitrary initials to identify the people in my life.

THE BLUE THAT REMINDS ME OF
THE BOAT WHEN SHE LEFT

Folds on your shirt lie like shadows
who hide me before she's leaving
You know she's leaving. The flag signals
us to mask and cross a plank so that
the transition will be easier, less visual
The sun has moved a bit and
sadness takes on new shapes
You say "Her shape sleeps in me and
the world explodes around her until
every atom resembles the match trick
she taught us last night"
We translated the dream before she left
then waited in the park by the dock
under shadows that were increasing
on your shirt as the sun grew feeble
Now she sends us postcards of sky & sea that say:
"I have had crazy dreams lately! Last night
I was dead and my skin was the color of this picture."

ANNE WALDMAN   197

"WHENEVER I MAKE A NEW POEM"

Whenever I make a new poem,
the old ones sound like gibberish.
How can they ever make sense in a book?

Let them say:

"He seems to have lived in the mountains.
He traveled now and then.
When he appeared in cities,
he was almost always drunk.

"Most of his poems are lost.
Many of those we have were found in
letters to his friends.

"He had a very large number of friends."

"I KNOW A MAN'S SUPPOSED TO HAVE HIS HAIR CUT SHORT"

I know a man's supposed to have his hair cut short,
but I have beautiful hair.
I like to let it grow into a long bronze mane.

In my boots.   In my blue wool shirt.
With my rifle slung over my shoulder
among huge boulders in the dark ravine,

I'm the ghost roan stallion.
Lief Erikson.
The beautiful Golden Girl!

In summer I usually cut it all off.
I do it myself, with scissors and a
little Jim Beam.

How disappointed everybody is.

Months and months go by before they can
worry about my hairdo
and the breeze
is so cool

FOR C.

I wanted to bring you this Jap iris
Orchid-white with yellow blazons
But I couldn't face carrying it down the street
Afraid everyone would laugh
And now they're dying of my cowardice.

Abstract beauty in the garden
In my hand, in the street it is a sign
A whole procession of ithyphallic satyrs
Through a town whose people like to believe:
"I was made like Jesus, out of Love; my daddy was
      a spook."

The upright flower would scare them. "What's shot,"
They think, "From the big flesh cannon will decay."
Not being there I can't say that being born is a chance
To learn, to love and to save each other from ourselves:
Live ignorance rots us worse than any grave.

And lacking the courage to tell you, "I'm here,
Such as I am; I need you and you need me"
Planning to give you this flower instead—
Intending it to mean "This is really I, tall, slender,
Perfectly formed"—is uglier than their holy fantasies,

Worse to look at than my own gross shape.
After all this fuss about flowers I walked out
Just to walk, not going to see you (I had nothing
         to bring—
This poem wasn't finished, didn't say
What was on my mind; I'd given up)

I saw bushes of crimson rhododendron, sparkling wet
Beside the hospital walk—I had to see you.
If you were out, I'd leave these flowers.
Even if I couldn't write or speak
At least I broke and stole that branch with love.

20:vii:58, ON WHICH I RENOUNCE THE NOTION OF SOCIAL RESPONSIBILITY

The minute I'm out of town
My friends get sick, go back on the sauce
Engage in unhappy love affairs
They write me letters & I worry

Am I their brains, their better sense?

All of us want something to do.

    I am breathing. I am not asleep.

    In this context: Fenellosa translated *No*
        (Japanese word) as "accomplishment"

                (a pun for the hip?)

Something to do

    "I will drag you there by the hair of your head!"
    & he began doing just that to his beautiful wife
    Until their neighbors (having nothing better to do)
    Broke it up

If nothing else we must submit ourselves
To the charitable impulses of our friends
Give them a crack at being bodhisattvas
    (although their benevolence is a heavy weight
        on my head
    their good intentions an act of aggression)

Motion of shadows where there's neither light nor
       eye to see
Mind a revolving door
My head a falling star

I shall know better next time than to drink with any
but certified drunks (or drinker) that is to say like
J-L. K. who don't fade away with the first false showing
of dawn through the Doug-fir & hemlock now here
Cornell Road First of Autumn Festival

    a mosquito-hawk awakened by my borrowed kitchen
    light scrabbles at the cupboard door
& the rain (this is Portland) all over the outdoor scene—
let it—I'm all in favor of whatever the nowhere gray
overhead sends—which used (so much, so thoroughly)
to bug me

                Let it (Shakespeare) come down
                   (& thanks to Paul Bowles for
reminding me)
there it rains & here—long after rain has stopped—
continues from the sodden branch needles—to rain,
equated, identified with nowhere self indulgence drip
off the caves onto stone drizzle mist among fern
puddles—so in a manner of speaking (Henry James
tells us)   "There we are."
the booze (except for a hidden inch or so of rosé in the
kitchen jug) gone & the cigarets few—I mean where IS
everybody & they are (indisputably) very sensibly abed
& asleep—

    one car slops by fast on overhead Cornell Road the

fireplace pops I wouldn't have anything else just now
except the rest of the wine & what am I trying to prove
& of course nothing but the sounds of water & fire &
refusing to surrender to unconsciousness as if that were
the END of everything—Goodbye, goodbye, at last I'm
tired of this & leave you wondering why anybody has
bothered to say "The sun is rising" when there's a solar
ephemeris newly printed, it makes no difference—but
you will be less than nowhere without this pleasurable
& instructive guide.

SOMETHING NICE ABOUT MYSELF

Lots of people who no longer love each other
Keep on loving me
& I

I make myself rarely available.

TRUE CONFESSIONS

My real trouble is
People keep mistaking me
    for a human being

Olson (being a great poet) says
"Whalen!—that Whalen is a— a—
That Whalen is a great big vegetable!"

He's guessing exactly in the right direction.

A POEM FOR TEA HEADS

I sit in Lees.   At 11.40 P.M. with
Jimmy the pusher. He teaches me
Ju Ju.

       Hot on the table before us
shrimp foo yong, rice and mushroom
chow yuke.

       Up the street under the wheels
of a strange car is his stash—The ritual.
We make it.   And have made it,
for months now together after midnight.
Soon I know the fuzz will inter-
rupt will arrest Jimmy and
I shall be placed on probation.

             The poem
does not lie to us. We lie under its
law, alive in the glamor of this hour
able to enter into the sacred places
of his dark people, who carry secrets
glassed in their eyes and hide words
      under the roofs of their mouth.

From A POEM FOR PAINTERS

      Our age bereft of nobility
How can our faces show it?
I look for love.
      My lips stand out
dry and cracked with want
              of it.
                    Oh it is well.

Again we go driven by forces
we have no control over. Only
                  in the poem
comes an image—that we rule
           the line by the pen
in the painter's hand one foot
            away from me.

Drawing the face
            and its torture.
That is why no one dares tackle it.
Held as they are in the hands
         of forces
      they cannot understand.
         That despair
is on my face and shall show
in the fine lines of any man.

I held love once in the palm of my hand.
        See the lines there.
            How we played
its game, are playing now
in the bounds of white and heartless fields.
        Fall down on my head,
love, drench my flesh in the streams
        of fine sprays. Like
                French perfume
        so that I light up as
            morning glorys and
I am showered by the scent
        of the finished line.

A POEM FOR THE INSANE

The 2nd afternoon I come
back to the women of Munch.
Models with god over

their shoulders, vampires,
the heads are down and
blood is the water-
color they use to turn on.
The story is not done.
There is one wall
left to walk. Yeah

Afterwards—Nathan
gone, big Eric busted,
Swanson down. It is
right, the Melancholy
on the Beach. I do not
                    split

I hold on to the demon
tree, while shadows drift
around me. Until at last
there is only left the
Death Chamber. Family Reunion
in it. Rocking chairs and

who is the young man
who sneaks out thru
the black curtain, away
from the bad bed.

Yeah stand now
on the new road, with the
huge mountain on your
right out of the mist

the bridge before me,
the woman waiting
with no mouth, waiting
for me to kiss it on.

I will. I will walk with
my eyes up on you for
ever. We step into
the Kiss, 1897.
The light streams.

Melancholy carries
a red sky and our dreams
are blue boats
no one can bust or
blow out to sea.
We ride them
and Tingel-Tangel
in the afternoon.

LETTERS,
ENCOUNTERS,
& STATEMENTS
ON POETICS

DONALD ALLEN

Although I had had some editorial experience of Jack Kerouac's *On the Road* as early as 1954 and 1955, when I had copyedited the "Jazz of the Beat Generation" episode for *New World Writing*, and had read the whole ms for a publisher, I did not get to meet him until late November or early December of 1956 when he and Allen Ginsberg came to my apartment at 59 West 9th Street in the Village. At the time I was putting together the second, "San Francisco Scene," issue of *Evergreen Review*, and Allen and Jack gave me mss and filled me in on recent developments on the West Coast.

During the next three years Jack sent me poems for *Evergreen Review* and for the anthology, *The New American Poetry*, I was editing in 1959. In the end we decided to print choruses from *Mexico City Blues* chosen by Allen plus Jack's biographical note and brief statement of his poetics. Later, in 1961, when I'd moved to San Francisco, Jack sent me his *San Francisco Blues* for a projected volume which never got off the ground.

His Mémère, Gabrielle, I first met when Barney Rosset entertained Jack and his mother and his French editors, Claude Gallimard and Michel Mohrt, at a luncheon party in 1958. And in the late spring of 1959, when I'd returned from a trip through South America, I accepted Jack's invitation and traveled to Northport for an overnight visit. Jack showed me his writing room and we talked at length about his unpublished mss and the origins of the Beat Generation. Mémère served a delicious and hearty supper which we ate at a round captain's table in the comfortable kitchen. Jack and I made a short foray to a nearby liquor store and bar and then we all turned in at a fairly early hour, they to watch TV in their bedrooms and I to sleep in the guest room.

WILLIAM BURROUGHS

From *Junky*

I once kicked a junk habit with weed. The second day off junk I sat down and ate a full meal. Ordinarily, I can't eat for eight days after kicking a habit.

Weed does not inspire anyone to commit crimes. I have never seen anyone get nasty under the influence of weed. Tea heads are a sociable lot. Too sociable for my liking. I cannot understand why the people who claim weed causes crimes do not follow through and demand the outlawing of alcohol. Every day, crimes are committed by drunks who would not have committed the crime sober.

There has been a lot said about the aphrodisiac effect of weed. For some reason, scientists dislike to admit that there is such a thing as an aphrodisiac, so most pharmacologists say there is "no evidence to support the popular idea that weed possesses aphrodisiac properties." I can say definitely that weed is an aphrodisiac and that sex is more enjoyable under the influence of weed than without it. Anyone who has used good weed will verify this statement.

You hear that people go insane from using weed. There is, in fact, a form of insanity caused by excessive use of weed. The condition is characterized by ideas of reference. The weed available in the U.S. is evidently not strong enough to blow your top on and weed psychosis is rare in the States. In the Near East, it is said to be common. Weed psychosis corresponds more or less to delirium tremens and quickly disappears when the drug is withdrawn. Someone who smokes a few cigarettes a day is no more likely to go insane than a man who takes a few cocktails before dinner is likely to come down with the D.T.'s.

Orlovsky was the kind of natural voice W.C.W. believed America would one day sound. I remember him praising Peter's first poem: "Nothing English about it—pure American." That was twenty years ago. Now, twenty years hence, Peter has voiced a volume of poems, pure Americana, and unlike any American sound. Bucolic and sexual, these poems are replicate of his farmer produce (organic and natural) and of his love for the male and female of his heart's desire.

He hails the human asshole as divine—He offers humankind an anatomical compassion for that bodily part long maligned, shame-wracked, and poetically neglect.

Keep it clean in between is a golden define of self-respect. The angel without wings is with asshole a reality. The angel with wings is a painted thing, a dream. The dual asshole: bucolic and sexual. What comes out, he believes, aught benefit the fields not the seas, aught fertilize not pollute—

What goes in, he lauds as a variable of sex not solely of homosexual kind—

The lovers of callipygian joy are universal.

Peter is an *original*; a refined spirit ... regard: 'neath his poetic capote nothing *primitive* holds claim—An agricultural romantic, the Shellean farmer astride his Pegasusian tractor repoems the earth with trees of berry and roots of honey; whose dirtian hands scribe verses of soy, odes of harvest; whose hymns to redolent shovels of manure nourish the fields that so nourish us, both in body meal and the cosmetics of soul.

LAWRENCE FERLINGHETTI

... I am put down by Beat natives who say I cannot be beat and "committed" at the same time, like in this poem ["Tentative Description of a Dinner Given to Promote the Impeachment of President Eisenhower"], man. True, true, William Seward Burroughs said, "Only the dead and the junkie don't care—they are inscrutable." I'm neither. Man. And this is where all the tall droopy corn about the Beat Generation and its being "existentialist" is as phoney as a four-dollar piece of lettuce. Because Jean-Paul Sartre cares and has always hollered that the writer especially should be committed. *Engagement* is one of his favorite dirty words. He would give the horse laugh to the idea of Disengagement and the Art of the Beat Generation. Me too. And that Abominable Snowman of modern poetry, Allen Ginsberg, would probably say the same. Only the dead are disengaged. And the wiggy nihilism of the Beat hipster, if carried to its natural conclusion, actually means the death of the creative artist himself. While the "noncommitment" of the artist is itself a suicidal and deluded variation of this same nihilism.

ALLEN GINSBERG

From *Notes for "Howl and Other Poems"*

By 1955 I wrote poetry adapted from prose seeds, journals, scratchings, arranged by phrasing or breath groups into little short-line patterns according to ideas of measure of American speech I'd picked up from W. C. Williams' imagist preoccupations. I suddenly turned aside in San Francisco, unemployment compensation leisure, to follow my romantic inspiration—Hebraic-Melvillian bardic breath. I thought I wouldn't write a *poem*, but just write what I wanted to without fear, let my imagination go, open secrecy, and scribble magic lines from my real mind—sum up my life—something I wouldn't be able to show anybody, write for my own soul's ear and a few other golden ears. So the first line of *Howl*, "I saw the best minds," etc. the whole first section typed out madly in one afternoon, a huge sad comedy of wild phrasing, meaningless images for the beauty of abstract poetry of mind running along making awkward combinations like Charlie Chaplin's walk, long saxophone-like chorus lines I knew Kerouac would hear *sound* of—taking off from his own inspired prose line really a new poetry.

I depended on the word "who" to keep the beat, a base to keep measure, return to and take off from again onto another streak of invention: "who lit cigarettes in boxcars boxcars boxcars," continuing to prophesy what I really knew despite the drear consciousness of the world: "who were visionary indian angels." Have I really been attacked for this sort of joy? So the poem got serious, I went on to what my imagination believed true to Eternity (for I'd had a beatific illumination years before during which I'd heard Blake's ancient voice & saw the universe unfold in my brain), & what my memory could reconstitute of the data of celestial experience.

But how sustain a long line in poetry (lest it lapse into prosaic)? It's natural inspiration of the moment that keeps it moving, disparate thinks put down together, shorthand notations of visual imagery, juxtapositions of hydrogen juke-box—abstract haikus sustain the mystery & put iron poetry back into the line: the last line of *Sunflower Sutra* is the extreme, one stream of single word associations, summing up. Mind is shapely, Art is shapely. Meaning Mind practiced in spontaneity invents forms in its own image & gets to Last Thoughts. Loose ghosts wailing for body try to invade the bodies of living men. I hear ghostly Academics in Limbo screeching about form.

JACK KEROUAC

The New American Poetry

The new American poetry as typified by the SF
Renaissance (which means Ginsberg, me, Rexroth,
Ferlinghetti, McClure, Corso, Gary Snyder, Philip
Lamantia, Philip Whalen, I guess) is a kind of new-
old Zen Lunacy poetry, writing whatever comes into
your head as it comes, poetry returned to its origin,
in the bardic child, truly ORAL as Ferling said, instead
of gray faced Academic quibbling. Poetry & prose had
for long time fallen into the false hands of the false.
These new pure poets confess forth for the sheer joy
of confession. They are CHILDREN. They are also
childlike graybeard Homers singing in the street. They
SING, they SWING. It is diametrically opposed to
the Eliot shot, who so dismally advises his dreary
negative rules like the objective correlative, etc. which
is just a lot of constipation and ultimately emasculation
of the pure masculine urge to freely sing. In spite of
the dry rules he set down his poetry is itself sublime.
I could say lots more but aint got time or sense. But
SF is the poetry of a new Holy Lunacy like that of
ancient times (Li Po, Hanshan, Tom O Bedlam, Kit
Smart, Blake) yet it also has that mental discipline
typified by the haiku (Basho, Buson), that is, the discip-
line of pointing out things directly, purely, concretely,

224

no abstractions or explanations, wham wham the true blue song of man.

Biographical Résumé, Fall 1957

When I was 4 my brother Gerard was 9, at his deathbed several nuns took down his last words about Heaven and went away with the notes, which I've never seen. They said he was a little saint. My father was a printer, in his plant I often made little one page newspapers, typesetting them and printing them on a hand press (Racetrack News).

I wrote my first novel at age 11, in a 5¢ notebook, about an orphan boy running away, floating down a river in a boat ... I went to parochial school in little black stockings and pants (St. Louis de France & St. Joseph in Lowell Mass). In high school, football, which led me (via scouts) to Columbia varsity but I quit football to write (because one afternoon, before scrimmage, I heard Beethoven fifth symphony and it had begun to snow and I knew I wanted to be a Beethoven instead of an athlete) ... First serious writing at 18, influenced by Hemingway and Saroyan and Whitman ... Spent 3 years on first full novel (1100-page Town and City) which was cut to 400 pages by Harcourt-Brace and thereby reduced from a mighty (overlong, windy, but sincere) black book of sorrows into a "saleable" ordinary novel ... (Never again editorship for me.) My father died in my arms in 1946, alone in house with me, told me to take care of my mother, which I do. After Town and City, I wrote On the Road but it was rejected (1951) so spent 6 years on the road writing whatever came into my head, hopping freights, hitchhiking, working as railroad brakeman, deck hand and scullion on merchant ships, hundreds of assorted jobs, government fire look-out. Slept in mountains and desert in my sleepingbag. My chief activity (seriously) is praying that all living things and all things may go to Heaven. It is said in ancient sutras, that if this prayer and wish is sincere, the deed is already accomplished. I'll buy that.

In recent reading appearance at Village Vanguard I was universally attacked, but all I did was stand there and read my heart out, not caring how I looked or what anybody thought, and I am satisfied because the dishwasher (an old Negro named Elton Stratton) said: "All I wanta do is get 2 quarts of whiskey and lie down in bed and listen to you read to me." Also, the musicians (Lee Konitz, Billy Bauer, Wilbur Little) said I was "sing-ing" when I read and said they heard the music, and since I consider myself a jazz poet, I am satisfied with that. What intelligentsia says makes little difference, as I've always spent my time in skid row or in jazz joints or with personal poet madmen and never cared what "intelligentsia" thinks. My love of poetry is love of joy.

I have been writing my heart out all my life, but only getting a living out of it now, and the attacks are coming in thick. A lot of people are mad and jealous and bitter and I only hope they also can be heard by an expanding publishing program the size of Russia's. Because it's not a question of the merit of art, but a question of spontaneity and sincerity and joy I say. I would like everybody in the world to tell his full life confession and tell it HIS OWN WAY and then we'd have something to read in our old age, instead of the hesitations and cavilings of "men of letters" with blear faces who only alter words that the Angel brought them . . .

As a child, I made long Chaplinesque movies by myself, taking all the parts, silent movies: I began doing this at age 5. Now I write them.

I am only a jolly storyteller and have nothing to do with politics or schemes and my only plan is the old Chinese Way of the Tao: "avoid the authorities." I am a bibulous old jolly drunk and I love everybody.

*

Don

My only possible statement on poetics and poetry is this: Add alluvials to the end of your line when all is exhausted but something has to be said for some specified irrational reason, since reason can never win out, because poetry is NOT a science. The rhythm of how you decide to "rush" yr statement determines the rhythm of the poem, whether it is a poem in verse-separated lines, or an endless one-line poem called prose ... (with its paragraphs).

So let there be no equivocation about statement, and if you think this is not hard to do, try it. You'll find that your lies are heavier than your intentions. And your confessions lighter than Heaven.

Otherwise, who wants to read?

I myself have difficulty covering up my bullshit lies

Jack

Belief & Technique for Modern Prose

List of Essentials

1. Scribbled secret notebooks, and wild typewritten pages, for yr own joy
2. Submissive to everything, open, listening
3. Try never get drunk outside yr own house
4. Be in love with yr life
5. Something that you feel will find its own form
6. Be crazy dumbsaint of the mind
7. Blow as deep as you want to blow
8. Write what you want bottomless from bottom of the mind
9. The unspeakable visions of the individual
10. No time for poetry but exactly what is

11. Visionary tics shivering in the chest
12. In tranced fixation dreaming upon object before you
13. Remove literary, grammatical and syntactical inhibition
14. Like Proust be an old teahead of time
15. Telling the true story of the world in interior monolog
16. The jewel center of interest is the eye within the eye
17. Write in recollection and amazement for yourself
18. Work from pithy middle eye out, swimming in language sea
19. Accept loss forever
20. Believe in the holy contour of life
21. Struggle to sketch the flow that already exists intact in mind
22. Dont think of words when you stop but to see picture better
23. Keep track of every day the date emblazoned in yr morning
24. No fear or shame in the dignity of yr experience, language & knowledge
25. Write for the world to read and see yr exact pictures of it
26. Bookmovie is the movie in words, the visual American form
27. In Praise of Character in the Bleak inhuman Loneliness

28. Composing wild, undisciplined, pure, coming in from under, crazier the better
29. You're a Genius all the time
30. Writer-Director of Earthly movies Sponsored & Angeled in Heaven

As ever, Jack

FRANK O'HARA

Personism: A Manifesto

Everything is in the poems, but at the risk of sounding like the poor wealthy man's Allen Ginsberg I will write to you because I just heard that one of my fellow poets thinks that a poem of mine that can't be got at one reading is because I was confused too. Now, come on. I don't believe in god, so I don't have to make elaborately sounded structures. I hate Vachel Lindsay, always have; I don't even like rhythm, assonance, all that stuff. You just go on your nerve. If someone's chasing you down the street with a knife you just run, you don't turn around and shout, "Give it up! I was a track star for Mineola Prep."

That's for the writing poems part. As for their reception, suppose you're in love and someone's mistreating (*mal aimé*) you, you don't say, "Hey, you can't hurt me this way, I care!" you just let all the different bodies fall where they may, and they always do may after a few months. But that's not why you fell in love in the first place, just to hang onto life, so you have to take your chances and try to avoid being logical. Pain always produces logic, which is very bad for you.

I'm not saying that I don't have practically the most lofty ideas of anyone writing today, but what difference does that make? They're just ideas. The only good thing

231

about it is that when I get lofty enough I've stopped thinking and that's when refreshment arrives.

But how can you really care if anybody gets it, or gets what it means, or if it improves them. Improves them for what? For death? Why hurry them along? Too many poets act like a middle-aged mother trying to get her kids to eat too much cooked meat, and potatoes with drippings (tears). I don't give a damn whether they eat or not. Forced feeding leads to excessive thinness (effete). Nobody should experience anything they don't need to, if they don't need poetry bully for them. I like the movies too. And after all, only Whitman and Crane and Williams, of the American poets, are better than the movies. As for measure and other technical apparatus, that's just common sense: if you're going to buy a pair of pants you want them to be tight enough so everyone will want to go to bed with you. There's nothing metaphysical about it. Unless, of course, you flatter yourself into thinking that what you're experiencing is "yearning."

Abstraction in poetry, which Allen [Ginsberg] recently commented on in *It Is*, is intriguing. I think it appears mostly in the minute particulars where decision is necessary. Abstraction (in poetry, not in painting) involves personal removal by the poet. For instance, the decision involved in the choice between "the nostalgia *of* the infinite" and "the nostalgia *for* the infinite" defines an attitude towards degree of abstraction. The nostalgia *of* the infinite representing the greater degree of abstraction, removal, and negative capability (as in Keats and Mallarmé). Personism, a movement which I recently founded and which nobody knows about, interests me a great deal, being so totally opposed to this kind of abstract removal that it is verging on a true abstraction for the first time, really, in the history of poetry. Personism is to Wallace Stevens what *la poésie pure* was to Béranger. Personism has nothing to do with philosophy, it's all art. It does not have to do with personality or intimacy, far from it! But to give you a vague idea, one of its minimal aspects is to address itself to one person (other than the poet himself), thus evoking overtones of love without destroying love's life-giving vulgarity, and sustaining the poet's feelings towards the poem while preventing love from distracting him into feeling about the person. That's part of Personism. It was founded by me after lunch with LeRoi Jones on August 27, 1959, a day in which I was in love with someone (not Roi, by the way, a blond). I went back to work and wrote a poem for this person. While I was writing it I was realizing that if I wanted to I could use the telephone instead of writing the poem, and so Personism was born. It's a very exciting movement which will undoubtedly have lots of adherents. It puts the poem squarely between the poet and the person, Lucky Pierre style, and the poem is correspondingly gratified. The poem is at last between two persons instead of two pages. In all modesty, I confess that it may be the death of literature as we know it. While I have certain regrets, I am still glad I got there before Alain Robbe-Grillet did. Poetry being quicker and surer than prose, it is only just that poetry finish literature off. For a time people thought that Artaud was going to accomplish this, but actually, for all their magnificence, his polemical writings are not more outside literature than Bear Mountain is outside New York State. His relation is no more astounding than Debuffet's to painting.

What can we expect of Personism? (This is getting good, isn't it?) Everything, but we won't get it. It is too new, too vital a movement to promise anything. But it, like Africa, is on the way. The recent propagandists for technique on the one hand, and for content on the other, had better watch out.

PETER ORLOVSKY

How I write poetry & who I learned from

In 1957 Paris, hotel room I wrote my first 2 poems all alone taping that typewriter & haveing so much fun I couldent believe my ears. Wrote some more poems on the subway wile rideing to hospital work. Always carrey notebook & pen so I can drop on paper like a wandering hen a green egg, observations that tickle my eye-brain or memory ear or emotional snapshots that perkolates under my skin like a swim in November Pound or care-ing for a pet pig for a yr. & writting poem about it 2 yrs latter or 7 yrs latter as in Love Poem To A. J. Muste, a gigantic quite pasafist. I get a kick jotting spontaneous flashes at odd moments & places. Working on farm fields out side all days singing my lungs content, sing-ing & saying aneything that passes in my mind, 2 hour song just for tomato plants wile transplanting a diging holes for their root-toots. Corso tought me to recognize funney spaech word idea combinations, Ginsberg & Kerouac extended speach-word flow, Catullus natural talk in poems, Rimbaud for lightening gumption action like walking over Alps in winter, Dostovesky for com-passion to other souls, Garcia Lorca for extra fine picture word detail, Ginsberg for his vast scope of subject matter & discription, W. C. Williams for staying on the reality track, Appolinair for his loose idea grab zone space, young poets for their freshness & clearity, Kenith Koch for his spontaneous fast funney wit lines, Trungpa for his sudden surprise cycle lie poems, B. Dylan for his hights of capital deliverey, F. Villon for his compact storey poetry, L. F. Celine for his word excitment pitching boat loads of rasberry morphine like words. Lyric jumps of Mayakovsky, down to earth grabbing hold of Serge Essenin's swaying intestines of his hair. I would like to go on but I have to finish my first book of poems called Clean Asshole Poems & Smileing Vegetable Songs pub. by City Lights, SF & jaring apple juice & apple sause etc & some farm nut tree care work. To be continued latter. Thnak you.

ACKNOWLEDGMENTS

Thanks are due to the following copyright holders for their permission to reprint:

DONALD ALLEN: Prose piece beginning "Although I had had some editorial experience" by Donald Allen, from *The New American Poetry, 1945–1960*, copyright © 1999 The Regents of the University of California. Reprinted by permission of the University of California Press. AMIRI BARAKA (LEROI JONES): "Preface to a Twenty Volume Suicide Note", "Sex, like desire", "War Poem" and "Political Poem" from *The Dead Lecturer* by Amiri Baraka, copyright © by Amiri Baraka, reprinted by permission of Sterling Lord Literistic, Inc. RAY BREMSER: "City Madness" (from "Poems of Madness") by Ray Bremser. Copyright © 1965, 1986 Ray Bremser. Used by permission of Jeffrey Weinberg, Literary Executor. WILLIAM S. BURROUGHS: Excerpt from *Junky* by William S. Burroughs, copyright © 1953 by William S. Burroughs. Reprinted by permission of The Wylie Agency (UK) Ltd. GREGORY CORSO: "After Reading 'In the Clearing'", "Second Night in N.Y.C. After 3 Years" and "Writ on the Eve of My 32nd Birthday" by Gregory Corso, from *Long Live Man*, copyright © 1962 by Gregory Corso. Reprinted by permission of New Directions Publishing Corp. "Away One Year", "Poets Hitchhiking on the Highway" and excerpt from "Transformation & Escape" by Gregory Corso, from *The Happy Birthday Of Death*, copyright © 1960 by New

241

permission of Coffee House Press. PHILIP WHALEN: "20:
vii:58, On Which I Renounce the Notion of Social Respon-
sibility", "For C.", "Prose Take-Out, Porltand, 13:ix:58",
"Something Nice About Myself", "True Confessions",
from *Overtime: Selected Poems* by Philip Whalen, copyright
© 1999 by Philip Whalen. Used by permission of Penguin,
a division of Penguin Putnam UK. JOHN WIENERS: Excerpt
from "A Poem for Painters", "A Poem for Tea Heads" and
"A Poem for the Insane" Copyright © 1986 John Wieners.
Reprinted from *Selected Poems 1958–1984* with the
permission of Black Sparrow Press.

We would also like to thank Jeffrey Weinberg of Water
Row Press for his invaluable help with permissions.

INDEX OF FIRST LINES